Richard Tangye

Reminiscences of Travel in Australia, America, and Egypt

Second Edition

Richard Tangye

Reminiscences of Travel in Australia, America, and Egypt
Second Edition

ISBN/EAN: 9783337205317

Printed in Europe, USA, Canada, Australia, Japan

Cover: Foto ©Andreas Hilbeck / pixelio.de

More available books at **www.hansebooks.com**

REMINISCENCES

OF

TRAVEL

IN

AUSTRALIA, AMERICA, AND EGYPT.

BY

RICHARD TANGYE.

WITH ILLUSTRATIONS BY E. C. MOUNTFORT.

SECOND EDITION.

London:
SAMPSON LOW, MARSTON, SEARLE, & RIVINGTON,
CROWN BUILDINGS, 188, FLEET STREET.

1884.

[All rights reserved.]

HAVING made several voyages to Australia, I have often been asked how I managed to relieve the monotony of so long a period on the water. I have never felt this monotony, simply because on each occasion I have set myself something to do.

In Mr. Trevelyan's "Life of Lord Macaulay" it is stated that when returning from India that statesman set himself the task of mastering the German language, and accomplished it during the voyage. I did not attempt anything so ambitious, but during my last voyage I occupied the time in writing the following pages; and as they were written under many difficulties, I feel I may confidently rely upon the indulgence of those who may do me the honour of reading them.

R. T.

Gilbertstone, 1884.

THE RABBIT AND THE THISTLE.

CONTENTS.

CHAPTER I.—*At Sea:*—Early Troubles—Cabin'd, Cribb'd, Confin'd—Travelling Companions—"Ordered Abroad by the Doctor"—"In the Bay o' Biscay O"—Ship Stewards—Racing under Difficulties—A Selfish Amusement—Musical Discords—The Ship's Newspaper—Our Ship goes too Fast—Why Ship Captains are Tories—Ixion goes Mad—Burial at Sea—The Parson "quite at Sea"—A Congregation Guaranteed—Look Out for Sharks!—"Let the Soup pass, Sir"—The "Scarlet Lady."   Pages 2 to 20.

CHAPTER II. —*At Sea:*—"Working off the Dead Horse"—"Poor Old Man!"—"May your Shadow never Grow Less!"—The "Blatant Beast"—The "Generous" Gambler—A Fiery Celt—The "Classic" Dolphin—"Get your Letters Ready"—"A Man of Peace *now*"—Mixing his Degrees—Good enough for the Colonies!—"Now Fridolin was a Pious Youth"—A Bootless Errand — Cross Signals — Tristan d'Acunha — A Parson Wanted—"The Rolling Forties"—A Hot January Morning.   Pages 21 to 39.

CONTENTS.

CHAPTER III.—*In Victoria :*—The Black Death in Melbourne—Melbourne—Education—A Caustic Smile—"All Work and no Play"—"A New Way to Pay Old Debts"—"Happy Land" in Victoria—"Hush! prohibited"—An Opening for "Gentlemen"—"Hallelujah Claim"—The Black Spur—A "Soafler"—Comforting the Widow—Hard Fare—Pioneering—Lovely Marysville—The Five Deadly Poisons—Back to Melbourne. Pages 40 to 59.

CHAPTER IV.—*In Tasmania :*—Cologu-ial Smells—Launceston—A Tonsorial Palace—Harvest in February—The Land of Snakes—Der Dichter spricht—"The Dangers of the Seas"—"Sweet Vale of Avoca"—A Charming Village—Where's Falmouth?—A Lonely Burying-place—A Narrow Escape—Snakes!—"Scotched, but not Killed"—"Acres many, People few"—The Rabbit and the Thistle—Breaking the Pledge—Hobart the Beautiful—Jericho to Jerusalem *via* Bagdad—Farewell, Tasmania. Pages 60 to 79.

CHAPTER V.—*In New South Wales :*—Off to Sydney—"What d'ye think of our Harbour?"—A "Southerly Buster"—Oysters on Trees—A rather particular Couple—Mount Victoria—A Tremendous Leap—A wicked Parrot—"Bail up"—The Laughing Jackass—Let Sleeping Bull-dogs Lie—An Election in Sydney—Beer and Bible—Through Wagga-Wagga—In the Bush—Track-making—Sighing for Old England—"Tommy"—Albury and Wodonga, a contrast—The Bushrangers. Pages 80 to 100.

CHAPTER VI.—*In Australia :*—Victoria, Protection—The Dog, subsisting on its own Tail—Cabby over-rides the Tramway—His Profit was not "quite enough"—Protection with a Vengeance—"Quite right to Cheat the Government"—Free Trade, New South Wales—A Genuine "Native Industry"—How Population is attracted—A Prosperous Colony—Demand for Agricultural Labourers—"Young Australia." Pages 101 to 112.

CHAPTER VII.—*On the Pacific:*—Homeward Bound—Ten Months' Drought—Auckland—Fiji—Kandavu Harbour—A Fearful Voice—Sharks and Dark Skins—Dropping a Day—A Colonial Doctor—Man Overboard—Honolulu—A Square Meal—Dressmaking in Honolulu—A "Brownie"—"Yes, for a Dollar"—A Plague of Centipedes—A Bilious "Down-Easter"—Jefferson Brick, Junior—"Mister"—"A Personal Favour!"—Through "The Golden Gate"—Earning a Cent anyway. Pages 113 to 132.

CHAPTER VIII.—*In America:*—San Francisco—The Palace Hotel—Chinese Washermen—The National Habit—Flats and Sharps—Qualifications for a State Governor—John Chinaman in California—The Missing Link—Little Min-ne, a Chinese Bride—Am claimed as a Chinaman—Pacific Sea-Lions—The last of "Mister"—Across America—A Magnificent Country—The Noble Red Man—A Long Arm and Quick Eye—John Bright—A Tremendous Crash—The Trapper's Story—How Taurus "Meets the Train"—The Alkali Plains—Salt Lake City—"I guess I'll take your Gold"—Rock Groups—"No, Sah!" said Sambo. Pages 135 to 159.

CHAPTER IX.—*In America:*—"Eat and be satisfied"—Chicago—Niagara—Ruthless Desecration—"He must raise his Salary"—The "American Language"—The Hudson—The Celestial Harmonies—A Dealer in Justice—"Rich, but Honest"—"Dear" America—Baggage Arrangements—Philadelphia—The Centennial Exhibition—An Argument for Protection!—Artisans' Wages and Holidays—Protection doomed—Cadgers—Freedom, for Tongue and Foot—Something hot! Pages 160 to 178.

CHAPTER X.—*In Egypt:*—Suez—Hassan—Donkeys for Nine—The Languishing Nobleman—Backsheesh—Painting the Lily—Forced Labour, a painful Sight—Agriculture à la Adam—School Interrupted—In the Bazaars—The Jewellers—A Bridal Party—Sultan Hassan—Familiar Devils—Up the Great Pyramid—The Heaven-sent Stick—A Wash and a Shave—To Sakkara—A Great City—At Sakkara—Tomb of the Sacred Bulls—The Tomb of a High Priest—A Graphic Biograph—The Eternal Backsheesh—A Camelcade.   Pages 181 to 208.

CHAPTER XI.—*In Egypt:*—Pious Orgies—Howlers and Dancers—Miss Whately's Schools—"She only steals the Eggs now!"—In Shubra Avenue—A Useful Animal—A Morning Ride—Sultan Selim—"Sir, I am a Christian"—A Holy Fakir—A Statue four thousand years old—Irrigation—Venerable Orphans—Home to Vote.   Pages 209 to 225.

CHAPTER XII.—*In Egypt:*—Port Saïd—Hawkers—Bohemiennes—Marines—The last Unmarried Lady—The Harbour—A discerning young Arab—The Red Ribbon Army—"Once a Member, always a Member"—The Spider—"One must be civ-il!"—Our Blue Jackets.   Pages 226 to 237.

CHAPTER XIII.—*The Suez Canal:*—Arabi in Exile—A 'cute Governor—The French outwitted—"Thomas Cook and Son"—A Black-Guard—Tel-el-Kebir—The Land of Goshen—The Suez Canal—Lord Palmerston—Immense Traffic—Lake Timsah—Predictions—Red Tape—Absurd Restrictions—Lesseps' Position—A Suggestion—The Dual Control—Arabi Bey—Mutinous Conduct—Irregular Court-Martial—How Arabi recruited his Army—"L'etat c'est moi."   Pages 238 to 259.

CHAPTER XIV. — *Alexandria :* — Ras-el-Tin — The Forts — A Courageous Merchant — Alexandria in Ruins — Alexandria *not* Bombarded — Anglo-Indians — Brindisi—Quarantine.   Pages 260 to 268.

INDEX,   Pages 269 to 290.

LIST OF ILLUSTRATIONS.

PORTRAIT	Frontispiece
VIGNETTE	Title
RABBIT AND THISTLE	Page vii.
TERRA FIRMA	1
TENERIFFE	7
THE SPORTS	8
THE CAPTAIN	11
ASCENSION	17
CROSSING THE LINE. WHY, DON'T YOU SEE IT?..	19
SHARK CATCHING	20
THE BABY HIPPOPOTAMUS AT PLAY	21
BURYING THE DEAD HORSE	23
THE CLASSIC DOLPHIN	28
A COLONIAL PARSON	31
IN THE TROPICS	40
GOLD MINE	49
A BIG TREE	52
ON THE BLACK SPUR	55
THE LYRE BIRD	57
COLLINS STREET, MELBOURNE	59
THE DOCTOR CONTEMPLATES—A POEM	64
AVOCA	67
ST. MARY'S	68
FALMOUTH HOTEL	69
BURIAL PLACE	70
SUMMIT OF MOUNT WELLINGTON	76
VIEW IN HOBART GARDENS	77
OUR WAITER	79
STARTING	80
SYDNEY HARBOUR	81
COTTAGE AT MOUNT VICTORIA	85
GOVETT'S LEAP, BLUE MOUNTAINS	87
DESCENT TO HARTLEY VALE	88
THE LAUGHING JACKASS	90
THE AUTHOR SKETCHING	91
A BULLOCK-TEAM	94
A BUSH HUT	95
AN UP-COUNTRY TOWN	98
ABORIGINES OF AUSTRALIA	100, 101
THE PLATYPUS	112
SYDNEY HARBOUR—GARDEN ISLAND	113
A FIJIAN	117
THE KING'S SISTER	126

The Hotel, Honolulu	132
Going East	135
The Chinaman	142
Little Min-ne	143
Seal Rocks, San Francisco	145
The Last of "Mister"	146
The Eucalyptus	148
Salt Lake	155
Monument Rock	158
The Devil's Slide	159
"Where's your Passport?"	160
Under the Falls, Niagara	163
The Pallisades, Hudson River	166
John Scales, Justice of the Peace	168
A Dragoman	182
A Donkey Boy	184
The "Orient"	186
The Schoolmaster "abroad"	189
A "Peep"	190
"Bery Cheap, Sah!"	191
The Mosque of Sultan Hassan	193
Ascending the Great Pyramid	196
View on the Nile	198
The Sphinx	199
A Wash and a Shave	200
The Serapeum, Sakkara	204
Bas-relief, Tomb of Tih	206
A Camelcade	208
Prayers in the Desert	209
A Runner, or Sais	213
In Shubra Avenue	214
Water Carriers	215
The Tombs of the Khalifs	217
A Street in Bulak	219
A Holy Fakir	221
A Wrecked Ship of the Desert	223
Au Revoir!	225
In the Suez Canal	226
A Feather Merchant	227
Cetewayo Disguised as a Gentleman	236
A Fellow Passenger	237
Adenese Women	240
A Wet Ride	260
A Familiar Face	261
The End	268

AUSTRALIA.

TERRA FIRMA

CHAPTER I.

IT is commonly supposed by landsmen that the perils of ocean travelling are much greater than those encountered upon land. For my own part, I believe that, once on the open sea, there is no pleasanter or safer mode of locomotion than is to be found in a well-appointed sailing ship or steamer. I certainly was in much greater danger of being drowned while travelling on the railway between Bristol and Plymouth upon one occasion than I have ever known myself to be while on board ship. The autumn had been exceedingly wet, and the low-lying districts in Somersetshire had become flooded, causing the railway to be completely submerged for a distance of about three miles. The water reached to the floors of the railway carriages, while the locomotive in its progress made a great wave in front of the train. The wheels of the locomotive were 8ft. 10in. in height, and the fire-box was 6ft. above the ground. Boats accompanied the train on either side during its passage through the water. Certainly I have never felt in so much danger in the 60,000 miles of ocean travelling which I have had since then. Not that there are no dangers to be met with on the water, as I found to my alarm before I had fairly commenced my last voyage.

Our vessel lay three miles off the Hoe, at Plymouth, and we had engaged a large sailing boat to take us on board. When we had got half way to the ship, and had lost the shelter of the land, a fierce squall struck the sail and turned the boat over on its side, throwing us into a confused heap on its bottom. The boatman tried to lower the sail, but having tied it in a fast knot he could not do so, and had no means of cutting the rope. The rain came down pitilessly all the time, and the waves dashed over us, drenching us to the skin, darkness coming on in the meantime. For a few moments we almost gave ourselves up as lost, but fortunately the violence of the wind lessened, the boat righted itself, and we got alongside our ship, but were unable in the darkness and the rush of the water and the noise of the wind and rain to make ourselves heard. My companion and I had to climb up the rope-ladder attached to the ship, and to scramble over its side as best we could, in the confusion altogether forgetting to take leave of our friends who were in the boat below, and who were lost to sight the instant we got on to the deck.

On entering the saloon the contrast was very great. The big ship riding at anchor was as steady as the land we had just left. The saloon was brilliantly lighted, and the passengers who had joined the ship at Gravesend were sitting round the table engaged in various occupations; some were reading or writing, while others were playing at whist, or were engaged in conversation. Being new arrivals, there was considerable curiosity to see which cabin we should call our own.

To a man taking his first voyage the phrase "cabin'd, cribb'd, confin'd" is at once understood as he surveys the cabin, a portion of which is to be his home for a month or two. The first feeling is that it will be impossible to bestow all his belongings in the limited space at his disposal, but before he has been long on board things settle down into their places, and he almost begins to wonder what he shall do with all the room.

The first night on board ship is generally one of great confusion. The passengers seem to be in everybody's way; but immediately after leaving port the baggage is stowed away, the purser allots the seats at table, and everything goes on with the greatest regularity.

The passengers on board one of the great Australian ships form a perfect epitome of the great world ashore. The line of division is sharply drawn between the various sets or cliques. Many never condescend to notice numbers of their fellow-passengers during the whole voyage; but for the most part fraternisation becomes general after the first fortnight has passed.

A three months' voyage often enables a man to form a juster appreciation of the character of his fellow-passengers than many years' residence in the same neighbourhood would do on shore; hence it often happens that life-friendships of the warmest kind are formed on board ship. On steamers bound for the Colonies representatives of almost every class are to be found. Judges returning to their duties after a holiday all too short; colonial statesmen with sufficient time on their hands to allow of their formulating a policy to meet every conceivable combination among their parliamentary opponents; and squatters and merchants returning to the Colonies to look after their property or their business. These men are generally very much preoccupied, and their only anxiety appears to be to get as speedily as possible to their destination.

Another class is composed of clergymen and professional men taking a holiday, and generally speaking with every sign of great enjoyment; while two other classes are largely represented—viz., invalids in search of health, and young ne'er-do-wells sent to the Colonies under the mistaken idea of their being more likely to reform in a new country. The latter class is mainly composed of young fellows who have never been brought up to any trade or calling at home, and who, with their friends, seem to think that the Colonies are a sort of "Tom Tiddler's ground," where they can "pick up gold and silver."

These youths are sent out by their friends as a last chance, under what is known as the "private convict system," and I believe that a very small proportion of them ever take a position of respectability after landing in the Colonies. Nor is it to be wondered at, for on the principle of "birds of a feather," etc., these young men get together on the outward voyage, and all their previous vices become much intensified by the association. On the other hand, many young men of good character, going out to the Colonies in search of employment, and showing by their conduct during the voyage that they are self-respecting, and consequently trustworthy, have secured good appointments from colonial merchants before leaving the ship.

Those who take the voyage on account of impaired health mainly consist of men suffering from overwork, and invalids more or less affected with pulmonary disease. In the case of the former a long voyage is the surest remedy; and for those in the earliest stage of consumption it is generally found to be efficacious; but it would be impossible to devise a more cruel fate for such as are thoroughly affected by that fell disease than to send them out on a long voyage. The conditions are all against them; the draught in the saloon is always great, and there is a total absence of those little comforts and delicacies which consumptive patients so greatly need, and the lack of which is so sorely felt. Doctors who have never made a voyage little think to what a miserable fate they are dooming their consumptive patients when they order them to take a sea voyage. In five cases out of six these patients are sent out too late, and the voyage only hastens their inevitable end, while, if they had only been sent in the earliest stages of the disease, they would almost certainly have been restored.

I started on my first Australian voyage on a lovely day in the late autumn. The sun was shining brilliantly, and as there was very little wind we fondly hoped we should cross the Bay of Biscay without having to go through the disagreeable experiences usually met with there; but our hopes were rudely dispelled when, after two days, having fairly got into the bay, we found a strong " nor'-wester " blowing, with heavy seas and torrents of rain.

Our ship was a duplicate of the ill-fated " London," and the officers comforted us with the information that we were just on the spot where she had gone down a few years before.

The wind and waves had been increasing in force during the day; but at four o'clock, just as we were sitting down to dinner, a heavy sea burst 'tween decks with a great uproar, breaking through the doors leading from the main-deck to the saloon, swamping the nearest cabins, and completely scattering the dinner, dishes and all.

The stewards had a busy time of it for the next two hours in mopping and baling the water out, and in preparing another dinner. Many of us, however, preferred retiring to our berths, the weather in the meantime getting decidedly worse. Presently another sea was shipped, deluging our cabin, amongst others, and leaving us in perfect darkness; while the noise of the sailors tramping overhead, the smashing of crockery, and the falling of blocks and ropes, the shouts of the officers, and the continual roar of the storm, effectually banished sleep for the night. I gained, however, one valuable piece of information, for as a result of the storm I learned a certain cure for sea-sickness! I had been quite ill before the final burst, but the excitement from this cured me instantly.

During the night we travelled out of the storm into smoother water, and it was curious to note the effect of this improved state of affairs, and of the bright sunshine, in bringing fresh faces on deck.

The life of a steward on board one of these ships is not an enviable one. He has to be up at work at four o'clock, washing and scrubbing the saloon; to wait at table four times a day; to make the beds, and attend to the cabins; and to be generally useful amongst the passengers, rarely finishing before ten o'clock at night. Our steward was a very handy fellow. He informed me he had a brother in New Zealand in practice as a doctor, who wanted him to settle there, but he preferred "a life on the ocean wave." He strongly recommended us to bathe frequently in salt water, saying it "was good for the spin-ial orgins!"

TENERIFFE (from a sketch by J. Willis).

Eight days after leaving Plymouth we passed the Canary Islands, steaming between Teneriffe and Gomera. The weather was delightful, and we had a fine view of the famous Peak, which rises apparently straight out of the sea to a height of 12,000 feet. These islands form a province of Spain, and are volcanic in their origin. The last eruption was in 1824. The vegetable productions of the islands are very varied. Palms and tropical plants grow near the sea; higher up cereals are grown; above, laurels; and still higher, pines and the white broom. The islands also produce oranges, lemons, dates, sugar-cane, cotton, and silk.

The "Sports" (from a sketch by G. A Musgrave).

Soon after passing the Canaries the Tropics are entered; and some of us begin to feel, for the first time, what heat really is. Awnings are fixed, and preparations are made for various kinds of amusements, amongst which the most popular are quoits, a run with the hounds, jumping in sacks by moonlight, racing in sacks, etc.

The game of quoits is much in favour with those who can play it, but it is a most selfish affair, for half-a-dozen men monopolise the whole of one side of the deck—and that the best or upper side—and, beginning at ten in the morning, continue till the dinner hour.

These are the day amusements. In the evenings there are concerts, recitations, and occasionally theatrical performances. Some passengers are of a studious turn, and divide their time between reading, writing, and walking, while others—notably young men from the Colonies—recline at ease during the day and become lively at night, often perambulating the decks with heavy heels till the small hours of the morning, to the great discomfort of those sleeping below.

Our second-class fellow-passengers commenced the concert season by giving a very amusing entertainment in their saloon. The first piece on the programme was an "overture by the band"—the band being represented by a single concertina. The chairman, a jolly-looking old tar, tried three pieces, and broke down in all, amidst roars of laughter and calls for the chorus. An "ancient buffer" sang "My Pretty Jane," and a few other sentimental things, with looks of fond affection. Then came a solo by "Bones," and another sailor gave a song which recounted his many ailments. He said he had had "brownchitis," "scarlatina," "concertina," and "tightness in the chest." Then a melancholy youth ground out something about his love for a "Little brown jug," calling frequently for a chorus, the whole ending with "God save the Queen."

We had other concerts during the voyage, and it was noticeable that the peculiarity which is said to attend amateur performances on land was not absent with us, for our concerts were usually productive of anything but harmony—at any rate amongst the singers. Those who were first invited to sing usually had colds, and those who were free from colds often declined because they were not invited first. Even the singing of hymns at the evening service was more than once made the occasion of heated discussion.

Another mode of occupying leisure hours on board ship as soon as the passengers have fairly settled down for the voyage is to start a newspaper. A few of the passengers meet and choose an editor, and the general public are invited to send contributions to him. At the outset promises of help are very abundant, but, as a matter of fact, the work has to be done by a very few persons. The paper appears weekly, in manuscript, and is usually read aloud by the editor after dinner on the day of issue.

Sometimes it is agreed to have the paper printed on reaching the Colony, and when that is determined upon one or two individuals undertake the duty of passing it through the press, and of forwarding it to the various subscribers. As a rule the same persons rarely undertake the duty twice, for it is a very arduous and ofttimes thankless task.

Some of the more cautious subscribers object to paying in advance, or require guarantees for due delivery and for the proper performance of the work. On one occasion one of my companions undertook the work of preparing the paper for the press, and correcting the proofs; it took him nearly three weeks to do so, and I am sure he will never undertake a similar task. The colonial printer gave him a great deal of trouble, persisting in ignoring his corrections, and in " improving the text" by altering it according to his own ideas. One peculiarity of amateur authorship came out into strong relief in the printing of this paper—the number of quotations and of inverted commas was so great that our printer's stock was quite exhausted, and he had to send all round the city to borrow a sufficient supply.

THE CAPTAIN (from a sketch by G. A. Musgrave).

In a three months' voyage the advantage of having a genial captain is obvious, and in this respect we were most fortunate, for it was impossible for anyone to be kinder or more considerate. Our captain entered heartily into all our amusements and schemes for the relief of the monotony of the voyage, and was ably seconded in his efforts by his amiable wife.

Sometimes it did appear to some of the more eager and impatient of the passengers that the captain was fonder of being on the water than they were; for he had a great regard for his sails, and whenever the wind developed unusual energy had no hesitation in diminishing the rate of our progress by shortening sail. The first officer, perhaps with the rashness of youth, would crowd all sail during his watch before breakfast, but when the captain made his appearance an order to " Take in those sails " would be promptly addressed to the chief.

Our captain had made the voyage more than twenty times, and had very carefully studied and noted the meteorological signs in various latitudes. The sky seemed like a book to him, and often when we could see no indications of change—and it was wonderful how quickly changes sometimes came—he would rapidly make his arrangements, and was rarely caught by the most sudden of tropical squalls. Our first experience of one of these squalls was when we were fifty miles to the south of Madeira. The weather had been fine all day, but about five o'clock we were aroused by great activity on the part of the officers and crew, who acted as though they expected to be boarded by pirates. The sky had become cloudy, and we were told that a squall was expected. The captain stood at the stern and gave his orders to the first officer in a quiet manner, while the latter shouted them to the sailors, who at once began to climb and pull at the ropes, all the while singing their sea songs. In the meantime the wind had come up, and was blowing like a hurricane through the rigging, and then the rain came down in torrents. While this was going on we saw a ship at a little distance, also overtaken by the squall, and it was wonderful to see how soon they took in her sails—it was done in a twinkling. Our vessel rolled and pitched heavily, and everything looked wet and wretched; but the squall passed off almost as quickly as it came, and the sun shone out, and everything looked smiling again. Unfortunately, during the storm the wind changed right ahead.

Our captain was a Tory, as most long-voyage captains are. I have often thought it strange that it should be so, seeing that the whole purpose of a captain's life is to make progress on his voyage; but it would appear that, although he is always progressing, he invariably comes back to his starting point.

At dinner one day, happening to say I was from Birmingham, the captain said jocularly, "Oh, that's where all the shams come from!"

Now the captain hails from London, but his wife is an Irish lady, so I answered, "No, captain, the things known as Brummagem shams are like the Irish bulls, and are, for the most part, manufactured in London."

"That's so," said the captain's wife; "well done, Mr. Tangye," and the captain subsided.

Truly life on shipboard is a curious medley. Here is a picture of what went on one night. In the lower tier of cabins lies a young man in the last stage of consumption, and almost in the agonies of death; in a cabin just above him is another suffering from scarlet fever; within a few feet of these are mothers nursing their babies. Sitting in a corner of the saloon is another young man, also in the final stage of consumption, away from all his friends, and without a single acquaintance on board; in front of him are two card parties, one of them playing for money, and looking as eager about it as though dear life depended on success.

While all this is going on below, what might have been a tragedy is being enacted on deck, for the quartermaster went suddenly mad while standing at the wheel. The captain had just given him some instructions, but he did not seem to take kindly to them, and was inclined to be disputatious. Presently he said, with an oath, "I won't argue with you to-night, captain." The captain then ordered another man to take the wheel, when the poor fellow ran along the deck and fell forward, kicking vigorously. The captain, thinking the man was in a fit, summoned the doctor, who, after waiting till the patient became quieter, tried to persuade him to go forward with him. The man, however, suddenly sprang up and aimed a tremendous blow at the poor little doctor, who, fortunately, being cunning of fence, managed to evade it. He then chased the doctor around the deck, and would doubtless have thrown him overboard if he could have caught him. The first officer then came to the rescue and seized the lunatic, but, although a very strong man, the doctor and he were unable to hold him, and ultimately it took six men to carry him forward. At last they managed to secure him, as they thought, but in a very short time the sailors came rushing pell-mell on to the poop-deck, the maniac having got loose and begun to chase them with a long fork. It was some time before they could again secure him, but finally they succeeded, and put him into a strait-jacket.

In the morning the first officer went to see the poor fellow, who asked him to shake hands, but the officer declined. "Well, sir," said the man, "I saved all your lives last night, for if I hadn't put the ship about she would have been right into that other ship on the starboard bow!" Of course this was entirely a delusion, for there had been no ship there.

Soon after entering the Tropics on one of my voyages, one of the second-class passengers was taken ill, and died in a few hours; he had been suffering from an attack of *delirium tremens*. The funeral was arranged to take place at 7.30 on the following morning, and at the appointed time the body, which had been sewn up in sail-cloth, was placed on trestles on the main deck, opposite a port-hole, the "Union Jack" covering it. Presently the bell began to toll, while the clergyman and captain read the service for the dead, and when the latter came to the passage "We therefore commit his body to the deep," he looked at the sailors, who at once loosed the corpse, which, being weighted with iron, shot through the open port-hole into the water with a great splash. During the ceremony the engines were stopped.

The day following was Sunday, and it being a glorious day, with a perfectly smooth sea, it was arranged for the service to be held on deck, which was covered with an awning. One of the passengers had brought a set of hand-bells with him, and he and some others rang out a peal before the service, the effect being curious.

The water was of a beautiful purple colour, and the sky a deep blue, and some large white birds were lazily flying around the ship. Under these unusual circumstances, and with the solemn incident of the burial of the poor drunkard on the previous day, one would have thought that even the dullest minister would have felt a thrill of inspiration. Judge, then, of our surprise when the parson commenced talking to us about geology! Nor did he make the slightest reference to the scene around him during the whole sermon. He told us, incidentally, that miners had not yet succeeded in getting more than twelve miles deep! During the afternoon I ventured to ask him where the mine was situated of which he had spoken, as, happening to know something about mining operations, I was anxious to know how the miners managed to pump the water from a depth of twelve miles. He answered testily, "I was not speaking of any particular mine."

On one occasion a discussion arose as to the best means to be adopted to ensure the attendance of the working classes at church. The reverend gentleman told us that for his part *he* had no difficulty in getting people to attend his church—all classes and conditions of people came to hear him, and yet he took no special means to secure their attendance. Not being impressed with the parson's eloquence, we were at a loss to understand how it was that he was so successful, when far abler and more attractive men failed so conspicuously; but he vouchsafed no explanation. On arriving in the

Colony the explanation was forthcoming, for I found that our reverend friend was chaplain to a cemetery!

On another occasion the old gentleman preached a sermon in which he related an anecdote of a soldier who was mortally wounded on the field of Waterloo. One of the chaplains found the poor fellow, who showed him a Bible which he had always carried in his pocket, it having been given him by his mother on leaving home. "Doubtless," said the clergyman, "this young man, having served his country to the death, went straight to glory." Curiously enough, in the lesson for that day occurred the verse, "Love your enemies," etc., so during the day I asked him how he reconciled the verse with the idea of the red-handed soldier going straight to glory? The parson (who was an Irishman) replied, "Sure, the soldier was heaping *fire* on his enemy's head!"

ASCENSION (from a sketch by J. Willis).

In about eighteen days after leaving Plymouth we reached the island of Ascension, whose fine group of volcanic peaks formed a magnificent object from our steamer. The island is used as a sanatorium for the British Colonies on the west coast of Africa. It has an area of about thirty-five square miles, and produces an abundance of turtles, pheasants, peafowl, and eggs, while tomatoes, castor-oil plants, and pepper, are indigenous.

The first officer went ashore with a boat to take our letters, and to bring back some turtles for use during the voyage. Immediately the boat left the ship we saw a big shark following close in its wake, the brute's fin showing above the water until the landing-stage was reached. This gave us some concern, as sharks are very bold at times, and have been known to snap at a hand hanging over the side of a boat. We saw large numbers about the ship during our stay, and one of the passengers shot several of them with a rifle. One was quite near to the ship when shot, and on feeling the bullet leaped right out of the water, and was instantly attacked and doubtless devoured by its brethren on falling back into the sea. We also put out a hook baited with pork, and observed several of the sharks make attempts upon it; but they appeared to be very clumsy, for they repeatedly missed it. Presently, however, one fellow got the hook firmly into his mouth, and we hauled him in over the stern on to the poop. He dashed about madly, looked very vicious, and reared right up on end, when the sailors barbarously hacked his tail off. Soon he was hauled on to the main-deck and quickly despatched, his teeth being on sale at a shilling each in less than an hour afterwards. Three turtles were brought on board "all alive," and placed on their backs on the deck until they were required by the cook. They each measured 5ft. 6in. long by 3ft. wide, and 6ft. 8in. in girth, and each weighed about 330lbs.

One day we had very rough weather, with an occasional sea dashing over the deck, along which the dinner was brought from the kitchen. My steward quietly told me to take none of the turtle soup, and I obeyed. After dinner I asked him why he advised me to let the soup pass? He said that as they were coming along the deck a sea came over and washed half the soup out of the tureen, decidedly mixing what was left! Those who partook of the soup remarked that the cook had put rather too much salt to it; but they libelled that useful functionary.

CROSSING THE "LINE"—"WHY! DON'T YOU SEE IT?"

One of our fellow-passengers was an old German lady, who was returning from a visit to her fatherland. She was very lively, and informed us she had not told her husband she was returning by this ship, intending, as she said, "to catch him on de hop," but she did not know that the passengers' names were all sent on by the mail, which went faster than we did; so when we got to the port her husband, "Shemmy" (Jemmy), as she called him, had come out with the pilot, and was very near catching *her* on "de hop," for she was a very lively old lady. One morning, while we were in the Tropics, upon getting on deck, we found the old lady dressed from head to foot in scarlet! It was too much, with the thermometer at 101° in the shade, so a deputation waited upon her and begged her to shade her glory, for it was too overpowering.

SHARK CATCHING.

THE "BABY HIPPOPOTAMUS" AT PLAY.
(From a sketch by G. A. Musgrave).

CHAPTER II.

AFTER being a month at sea the sailors performed the ceremony called "Burying the Dead Horse," the explanation of which is this: Before leaving port seamen are paid a month in advance, so as to enable them to leave some money with their wives, or to buy a new kit, etc., and having spent the money they consider the first month goes for nothing, and so call it "Working off the Dead Horse." The crew dress up a figure to represent a horse; its body is made out of a barrel, its extremities of hay or straw covered with canvas, the mane and tail of hemp, the eyes of two ginger beer bottles, sometimes filled with phosphorus. When complete the noble steed is put on a box, covered with a rug, and on the evening of the last day of the month a man gets on to his back, and is drawn all round the ship by his shipmates, to the chanting of the following doggerel:—

BURYING THE DEAD HORSE.

Oh! now, poor Horse, your time is come; And we

say so, for we know so. Oh! many a race we

know you've won, Poor Old Man.

You have come a long long way,
   And we say so, for we know so.
For to be sold upon this day,
   Poor Old Man.

You are goin' now to say good-bye,
   And we say so, for we know so.
Poor old horse you're a goin' to die,
   Poor Old Man.

Having paraded the decks in order to get an audience, the sale of the horse by auction is announced, and a glib-mouthed man mounts the rostrum and begins to praise the noble animal, giving his pedigree, etc., saying it was a good one to go, for it had gone 6,000 miles in the past month! The bidding then commences, each bidder being responsible only for the amount of his advance on the last bid. After the sale the horse and its rider are run up to the yard-arm amidst loud cheers. Fireworks are let off, the man gets off the horse's back, and, cutting the rope, lets it fall into the water. The *Requiem* is then sung to the same melody.

> Now he is dead and will die no more,
>   And we say so, for we know so.
> Now he is gone and will go no more;
>   Poor Old Man.

Burying the Dead Horse (from a sketch by G. A. Musgrave).

After this the auctioneer and his clerk proceed to collect the "bids," and if in your ignorance of auction etiquette you should offer your's to the auctioneer, he politely declines it, and refers you to his clerk!

As we neared the Equator the heat became very oppressive. On October 2nd, when 7° north of the line, the thermometer stood at 120° in the sun, while under the awning it registered 85°. On the thermometer being dipped into the sea the temperature of the surface water was found to be 82°, while in the cabin at midnight the thermometer stood at 80°, with the wind blowing in at the open porthole.

In passing under the vertical sun the old proverb "may your shadow never grow less" is entirely out of place, for it is impossible it can diminish, unless, indeed, one should become like poor misguided Peter Schlemihl, and find oneself altogether without one! When standing upright my shadow was about two feet in diameter, and it looked like the shadow of the brim of my hat all round my feet.

The wife of the captain of our steamer had been very unwell until we had passed the Equator, and had not come out of her cabin. One evening, soon after she made her first appearance, I was chatting with her, when, finding I was from Cornwall, she asked me if I knew a certain watering-place in that county which she named. It happened that I had a residence at the place in question, and curiously enough she had been a visitor at the same house before I had it, and she said, "last year my sister was staying in the neighbourhood with some friends, when they were nearly caught by the tide on the beach opposite the house, and had to scale the face of the cliff, climbing up some old ladders left in an abandoned mine." I told her if they had taken my advice, and had turned back, they would not have had such an unpleasant adventure, for I happened to be on the beach at the time, and warned the party of their danger, but they disregarded it! It was curious to be reminded of this occurrence under such circumstances.

Amongst our fellow-passengers were two young men, whose friends, it was reported, had become tired of them at home, and had made a present of them to the Colonies. They were very lively youths, and did their best to keep the ship lively by their pranks and escapades. They were known by the names of "Tall and Fat," and "Short and Stout," and were always together. Sometimes, however, the playfulness of these two young men received an unexpected check. On one occasion they had gone "forward" to play some tricks upon the emigrants, who, however, did not see the fun; so, having got the lads into a corner, they covered them, first with molasses and then with flour, and so returned them to the saloon. They did not repeat their visit.

There is one feature on board many ships which always strikes passengers with surprise; and that is the impunity with which the "wild spirits" carry on their disorderly conduct. Drinking, betting, shouting, tramping the deck at unseemly hours of the night, are permitted, to the great annoyance of the majority; but it is in vain that you appeal to the officers—they will not interfere. On one occasion a noisy youth, who went by the name of the "Blatant Beast," was firing a revolver about "at large," and although we appealed to the captain, and begged that he would disarm the lad, it was useless—he would not interfere. Ultimately the young man accidentally discharged the pistol and broke his arm, and so relieved his neighbours from further apprehensions for a time.

One night "Short and Stout" and "Tall and Fat," and a few other rowdies, got drunk, and in their rambles found a poor harmless cat, which they chased all over the ship, and succeeded in killing. On the following day these gallant youths determined, in Irish phrase, to "wake" the cat. They proceeded to fit up one of their cabins as a chapel, and upon a bier the corpse of poor pussy was laid, having been dressed for the occasion, candles surrounding the body. The mourners, or murderers, stood around the body with pipes in their mouths, meggy-howling and cat-a-wauling in a most vigorous fashion, afterwards parading the deck, headed by one of their party, arrayed in a dress coat over a night shirt, and wearing a tall white hat, carrying the dead body of poor puss before him.

Betting is often carried on to a great extent, considerable sums of money changing hands. One passenger told me, after we had been some weeks at sea, that he had cleared enough to pay for his own passage, and also for that of his wife and child, and that it only remained for him to win enough to pay for the nurse, and to take them all from Australia to New Zealand, and he should be happy! I knew one man, the father of a very large family, who lost £700 in three weeks, £400 of it going at a single night's play; yet, with striking consistency, this open-handed gentleman refused to allow his wife and daughters to go on shore at one of the most interesting of our ports of call on the score of the expense, which he said would amount to at least £2 or £3!

A pleasant sight it is to watch the fish and birds which begin to make their appearance about 30° S. Occasionally flocks of flying-fish are to be seen flying a few feet above the water, pursued by dolphins. Sometimes their headlong flight carries them right on to the deck, or through the cabin windows when lighted up after nightfall. They are caught by the sailors at night by the simple device of suspending a net in front of a lantern, and they are said to be very good when cooked.

We first saw that splendid bird, the albatross, when about 28° S. latitude, and when more than 1,000 miles from land. They appeared in flocks, and would follow the ship for many days. Their flight is exceedingly graceful, and very rapid, the movement of their wings being scarcely perceptible. The capture of the albatross is a favourite amusement upon sailing ships—it is scarcely possible to catch them from a steamer—the plan being to let out a line over the stern, having a strong hook baited with a piece of meat or with red cloth. We were successful in catching a magnificent fellow, which measured 15ft. across its wings. A drop of prussic acid applied to the eye of the poor creature causes instant death. The breast forms an excellent muff, and the wing bones make good stems for pipes of the "churchwarden" pattern. One of our passengers was a fiery Irishman, who was travelling with his newly-married wife. One day, while at dinner, the ship gave a heavy lurch, and the lady fell back, breaking her chair; upon which her husband, in a great rage, seized the chair, and, rushing on deck, threw it overboard, when lo! a flock of albatrosses crowded around it, and one fine fellow "took" the chair, and appeared to be addressing his friends!

One of the most beautiful creatures to be seen in tropical waters is the "Portuguese Man-of-War." It is often confounded with the Nautilus, but is a quite distinct organism; it has a crest which can be raised or lowered at will, and its body consists of a long, horizontal, oblong bladder filled with air. They vary in size from 12in. diameter to small discs no larger than a shilling, and present a beautiful appearance as the ship passes by a fleet of them.

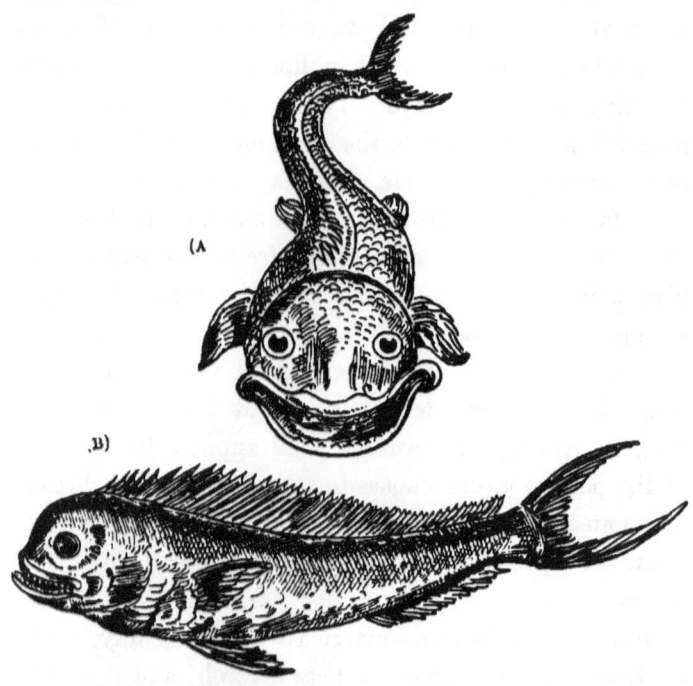

(A) The "Classic" Dolphin.   (B) The Dolphin.

We caught some dolphins, and an examination of their stomachs proved they were not unjustly suspected of eating the pretty little flying-fish. The pilot-fish, also found in these latitudes, is coloured purple and silver, with five black bands across it, and is about five inches in length. We also saw specimens of the white shark, porpoises, grampuses, Mother Carey's chickens, booby-birds, etc.

One of the most interesting sights at sea is the passing of ships. I shall never forget our meeting a ship in full sail one glorious moonlight night. It came close to us, the moon shining full on its sails, and being like our vessel, a sailing ship, not a sound was heard until our captain hailed the stranger, and asked him to report us " all well."

One would think there was not much danger of collision at sea, in broad daylight and in the open ocean, but on one occasion, while in a sailing ship, another came so close to us that it was only by the most dexterous management on the part of our captain that a collision was avoided.

The monotony of a long voyage is occasionally relieved by the opportunity of sending letters in homeward-bound ships, and when we had been out about a month we were told to have our letters ready, for a ship was in sight. Everyone was immediately deeply engaged in writing, and presently the stranger came sufficiently near for us to communicate with her. Our signal was run up, " Will you take letters for us?" to which she quickly replied, " With pleasure," and then a boat left us to take our letter-bag on board the " homeward-bound." This vessel was from Moulmein with teak, and she had been one hundred days out. Those on board had heard nothing of the Cabul massacre, but they brought us news of the capture of Cetewayo, having got it from a passing ship. In return for this intelligence we told them of the death of the Prince Imperial, which they had not heard of, although it happened before the capture of Cetewayo.

Some of our passengers went on board the passing ship, and two of them scrambled up the rigging, and presently we saw a sailor follow them and tie their legs to the rigging, releasing them as soon as they had paid their footing. In the evening the two ships parted company, saluting each other with rockets of various colours.

While our letters were being taken on board the homeward-bound ship, we saw a huge shark follow the boat until it reached the vessel, and on hearing a shout, "a big fish!" we ran to the ship's side and saw a whale not more than a hundred feet off. The monster gave a loud snort, spouted water, and then made off. I wonder if it had any idea what we were?

There was a boxing match going forward one day, when the captain invited the parson to put the gloves on. "Oh, no," he said, "I am a man of peace *now*." He told me he objected to war as much as anyone could do. "But," I said, "your Church does not." He replied that there was nothing in the teaching of the Church which advocated war; so I asked him, if that was the case, what that part of the prayer-book meant where a hope is expressed that the Queen may "vanquish and overcome all her enemies."

At dinner one day our friend undertook to explain to us how drain-pipes were made. He said, "You know those round things that are put in the earth to carry off the water?" Some one suggested drain-pipes. "Ah, yes," he said, "you know they take a kind of clay not like other clay, and put it into a sort of machine and turn it around and the pipes are made." I thought his description was not so good as that of the Irishman who explained the manufacture of cast-iron pipes by saying, "You take a round hole and pour the metal around it."

A COLONIAL PARSON (from a sketch by Wyburn).

Some one remarking that we were now 36° south, he said, "Ah, that is just 4° below freezing," having confused the degrees of latitude with those of the thermometer. Upon being told that 32° was the freezing point. "Really?" he said, "I always thought it was 40°"

In listening to most of the clergymen with whom I have travelled, I have been irresistibly reminded of the complaint made so bitterly, and with so much truth, by Australian importers in the early gold-finding days, that English merchants and manufacturers were utterly reckless as to the quality of the goods they sent out, acting on the principle that "anything will do for the Colonies." This idea has long ceased to have any currency, for it has been discovered that the coinage of the Australian mint ranks equally with that of London, but it does not appear that those responsible for the due supply of clergymen to the Colonies have realised the same truth, for on every hand I have had my own experience confirmed. The general complaint amongst the colonists, especially in the country districts, is that either young and totally inexperienced men are sent to them, or else men who have proved failures at home; and they not unnaturally resent such treatment.

In a recent voyage we had a large number of steerage passengers, and amongst them was a very earnest, hard-working evangelist from Mr. Spurgeon's college; this man had sacrificed his ease during the voyage by attending to the sick and ailing "in season and out of season," and was admitted on all sides to have done much good; frequently, too, he held religious services amongst the steerage passengers, and met with great acceptance. One man had been very ill for a long time, and had been tenderly waited upon by the evangelist. After a time he became suddenly worse, and some passengers at once went to a clergyman, who suggested that the Communion should be administered. Having obtained the help of another clergyman and two or three of the passengers—none of whom had before shown any interest in the patient—they proceeded on their errand without saying a word to the evangelist, and on the following Sunday the clergyman preached a sermon to the poor people, endeavouring to prove that no one had any right to teach or to preach but members of his Church, who, only, held the true commission, by virtue of what he called the "direct succession from Peter:" and I suppose he thought he was preaching religion, not perceiving that he lacked what Paul described as being the highest of all the Christian virtues—that of charity.

In passing through the Tropics one of the most glorious sights is the phosphorescence in the sea. Of course it can be seen to the greatest advantage in the absence of the moon; it is something wonderful, and worth coming all the way to see. As far as the eye can reach, the track of the vessel is marked out with the utmost brilliancy, and sometimes tiny balls of phosphorus seem to explode, scattering their radiance far and wide.

We had as fellow-passengers three young men who rarely spoke to anyone outside their own party, and during the early part of the voyage they usually sat on the deck for hours at a time engaged in reading their Bibles and making notes on the margin. After we had been out a few weeks the youngest of the three was stricken with scarlet fever, and at one time he was seriously ill.

The trio were known as the "Danite Band." The eldest was a young man about twenty-one, and one evening I had a little chat with him. He said he belonged to no sect; he had "come out from among them"— that his soul was safe, die when he would, and that he could only look on the poor sinners around him with a pitying eye, and pray for their souls. He was rejoicing at having saved one soul since he came on board. It so happened that this young man occupied the same cabin as the youth who was ill with fever, but becoming alarmed for his personal safety (not his soul's), he requested to be accommodated elsewhere, while another passenger volunteered to take his place and to nurse the invalid, so they exchanged cabins. On the following Sunday the young man who had volunteered as nurse knocked at the pious young man's door and asked for his boots, receiving for answer, "I won't be bothered about boots on the Lord's Day."

It is usual to hold a bazaar on passenger ships proceeding to or from the Colonies. These bazaars are almost invariably held in aid of the funds of the Merchant Seaman's Hospital and other similar institutions, and a large sum is annually obtained in this way. The result in the case of the sailing vessel in which I made one of my voyages was a sum of over £50, besides some annual subscriptions, although the number of adult saloon passengers was only about thirty.

Great preparations were made for this bazaar, it being the event of the voyage. The day previous the sailors were busily engaged closing-in the promenade deck with canvas and bunting, and dividing it off into stalls by means of flags and other coloured materials. While thus engaged, another sailing vessel came in sight, and the sea being nearly dead calm the two vessels approached closely, and parties were speedily passing to and fro. We invited some of the passengers in the stranger to join us to-morrow, and they invested about £5 in lotteries before going back for the night.

Next day was a most lovely one, but a heavy rolling sea was sufficient to prevent our visitors of yesterday joining us. Nevertheless, we thoroughly enjoyed the day ourselves, for the whole ship's company—passengers, crew, men, women, and children—held high carnival on the promenade deck. It was pretty to see the children of the second class, who, owing to the high bulwarks, were rarely able to see over the ship's side, rush first of all to look over the rail at the heaving sea.

The first officer was dressed as a showman, and presided over the Fine Art Exhibition, his face being painted a fine terra-cotta tint. The crew and stewards were variously costumed as nigger minstrels, etc. The stalls were presided over by the ladies, who, as usual, were very successful in disposing of the various articles, which, by the way, were for the most part made up by the ladies themselves during the voyage. Much curiosity was excited by the announcement of a dramatic performance, entitled "The White Squall," which was to take place in the Theatre Royal. The *corps dramatique* evinced great anxiety to secure the attendance of the whole ship's company, and were fairly successful. The performance did not take long, for as soon as the audience were seated cries of "Let go" were heard from the actors, upon which the air was filled with a veritable "White Squall," consisting of clouds of flour, causing a general stampede.

Next day we found our companion of yesterday lying at some distance ahead, while a stranger lay on the port quarter. A curious instance of cross-signalling ensued. The stranger asks our companion, the St. Vincent, for latitude and longitude. The St. Vincent missing this, and intent on their investment in yesterday's lottery, puts up, "What have we won?" The reply, "Nothing." The stranger runs up, "Don't understand. Repeat, please." Then St. Vincent replies, "Very sorry," upon which our Captain signals the stranger, and removes all further doubt.

We passed close to the Island of Tristan d'Acunha, which lies in the South Atlantic, lat. 37° 6′ S., long. 12° 7′ W. As a curious little history attaches to the island, I make the following extract from our ship's newspaper:—

"Tristan d'Acunha is a volcanic peak of very considerable altitude, so considerable indeed that its summit is covered almost perpetually with snow. It rises sheer out of the water, and there is only a single landing-place on the whole island. Previous to the downfall of Bonaparte it was uninhabited; but when that scourge was despatched to St. Helena, the British Government deemed it advisable to secure this isolated rock, and so prevent the French using it as a base of operations against the place of Napoleon's internment. A small company of soldiers, in charge of a corporal, was therefore despatched, and left in possession.

"In 1821 Napoleon died, and the necessity for maintaining the garrison at Tristan existed no longer. A man-of-war was accordingly sent to bring away the corporal and his little army. But he and they had by this time comfortably settled down, tilled the—rock we were about to say—and produced excellent potatoes and other vegetables; raised pigs and goats, and having in some mysterious way obtained wives, had raised families too. They were therefore extremely reluctant to leave the scene of their successful labours; and the English Government, nothing loth to encourage colonisation, at once gave the necessary permission to remain, and with it a small pension or annuity.

"They have gone on flourishing and increasing, forming a useful and peaceable community in the very centre of the South Atlantic; useful because whalers and other vessels, by putting in there, are able to obtain fresh potatoes, vegetables, and pigs. Little money is used, barter affording sufficient facility for interchange.

"Crime is almost unknown. We had as well said absolutely unknown, for it is doubtful whether the one case of dishonesty on record as such was not rather an ill-fared joke. It seems that when a marriage takes place a pig is killed by the bride's father, and dressed the night before the nuptials. On the occasion referred to the pig disappeared before morning, and was traced to the house of a notorious wag, as to whose fate history is silent. It is only fair to add that he admitted taking the pig, but protested that it had been done by way of a practical joke. At one time a missionary existed in the midst of this innocent community, but he eventually disappeared—either died or was removed. His place was never refilled, and the consequences have been rather trying to the budding men and women of Tristan, for whereas in the missionary's days loving couples could be, to use a nautical phrase, "spliced," when they had made up their minds, *now* they must wait until a chance man-o'-war, with a chaplain on board, puts in, and as their visits are nearly as rare as those of the angels, the patience of these Tristan lovers must unquestionably be sorely strained. When, however, like some comet of very eccentric orbit, the parson does at length turn up, he finds plenty of ripe pairs ready—nay, eager—for him.

"What a popular man that parson must be! Last and most interesting fact. When the 'Sobraon' put in at Tristan in 1879 the corporal was still living, a venerable patriarch of ninety years."

After leaving Tristan we soon get "into the forties," or as the sailors are wont to say, "the rolling forties," where the westerly winds steadily prevail, and continue right on until we make Cape Leeuwin. These winds cause the magnificent waves, or "rollers," which tower up over the stern of the vessel, threatening, apparently, to overwhelm it. In a gale of wind, and when the "following seas" are running at a high speed, it becomes necessary for some vessels to "lie to" in order to avoid this catastrophe. We had an opportunity of seeing this operation. Soon after passing the Cape we were overtaken by a heavy gale, and a high following sea. Our vessel being a sailing ship of the old type, with broad bluff bows, necessitated our adopting that course. Our stem was turned in the teeth of the wind and sea, and, with the exception of a top-sail and jib-sail, all our canvas was closely taken in. She lay so all night, labouring heavily, and the sea breaking over her decks.

Soon after sighting Cape Otway vessels bound for Melbourne receive their pilot, whose advent is the occasion of great excitement among the betting fraternity. Bets are laid on the colour of his hair and whiskers, whether or not he has a moustache, the letter with which his name begins, and which foot he will first put on deck. As soon as he makes his appearance he is greeted with shouts of "What's your name?" Evidently he is accustomed to it, for he does not look surprised. In this particular case everyone was out as to the colour of his hair and beard, for he had a black beard and white whiskers. The pilot brought news of a general election in one of the colonies, and one of our passengers, a colonial statesman, eagerly asked him for papers. The statesman's countenance was expressive of blankness within when he saw he was beaten in his constituency—but soon brightened on hearing he was returned by another.

The entrance to Hobson's Bay is very narrow, and the distance therefrom to Melbourne is about 40 miles. We landed soon after six on a January morning, and found the heat almost unbearable. Taking a cab to our hotel, we made our first experience of the high charges in a Protectionist colony, for we were obliged to pay a guinea for this service.

In the Tropics (from a sketch by the Author).

CHAPTER III.

WHEN driving to the hotel we were struck with the deserted appearance of the streets, as very few persons were seen during our three miles' ride from Sandridge. It did not occur to us that this arose from the earliness of the hour, our day having commenced about three A.M., when we began to make preparations for landing; but, as will be seen, the fact became of startling significance to us. While waiting for breakfast I took up the newspaper, and had not proceeded far before I came to an article headed "The Black Death in Melbourne." This article gave a detailed and circumstantial account of the progress of the disease, which was stated to have been raging for the past four or five weeks. Among other things, the article stated that the number of deaths had become so great that it was impossible to dig separate graves; that the bodies were placed in trenches, one being dug each day; that all who could leave the city had fled; and that the mob had surrounded the Town Hall, demanding to see the Mayor and Corporation, who, however, had already disappeared. Getting alarmed, we rang for the waiter, and asked him how we could get to Adelaide. He naturally enough seemed surprised, as we had only just arrived. I told him it was too bad he had not warned us of the state of the city, and of the existence of the plague. The man looked astonished. I asked him if there had not been great illness and mortality in the city. He answered that there had been a few cases of measles, and a whooping-cough or two, and that six people had died during the last week from these causes. I began to suspect we had been "sold," and was about to pass the paper to him when I caught sight of an asterisk placed against the heading, and on looking at the foot of the column saw that the article was written as a prediction of what would happen in Melbourne within 100 years unless sanitary matters were at once attended to.

Melbourne is a city of fine broad streets, handsome public buildings, splendid shops, and vast warehouses. Indeed, a stranger cannot fail to be struck with its metropolitan-like character. Only forty years ago the site on which it stands was a mere swamp with a few log huts; now its population is about the third of a million souls. For this population a series of educational institutions of an unusually high character have been founded, and are in active operation. The Free Library, which we visited, is a handsome room, and seems in every way well adapted to the requirements of a large number of students and readers. We were impressed with the quietude which prevailed, notwithstanding that the room was well filled with readers, most of them apparently of the artizan class. The Art Gallery is a free institution, and contains a very fair collection of good paintings.

The Natural History Museum, which by the way is really a museum of general science, is a truly magnificent institution. Very fine collections are here classified in a manner which, while perfectly lucid to the student, is also in strict accordance with the views of modern scientific authorities. We noticed particularly a good collection of sedimentary fossils, well preserved and fairly comprehensive. A fine meteorolite weighing 30cwts., a portion of one weighing four tons which fell in Victoria a few years ago, is a prominent object near the entrance. This museum, in common with the Art Gallery and Free Library, is the resort of vast numbers of students, and it is cheering to be informed that the working classes largely avail themselves of the advantages thus provided for them.

As in the other Australian colonies, education here has been taken up in a vigorous and thorough manner, and the State schools are a credit to the colony. Although the population of Victoria is under one million, we observed in Melbourne a school bearing the inscription No. 1465. But with all this liberality and foresight, a strange blot exists in the educational course, for the study of history is, in deference to the prejudices of a portion of the population, absolutely interdicted. It is impossible, however, that this absurd concession to ignorance can long be endured. In leaving Aden on one occasion I began to have doubts as to whether geography was also excluded, for a young man, son of a well-to-do squatter, hearing me speak of Suez, asked which end of the canal that town stood at; and another youth, in passing the island of Candia, said he always thought *Canada* was somewhere in America.

Happily, no fears exist in Australia as to the policy of thoroughly educating the people ; on the contrary, it is commonly recognised that the future prosperity of the State—indeed its very existence—depends upon the universal diffusion of education.

At the time of our visit party feeling ran very high in connection with the doings of the " Berry" Ministry, and as extraordinary personalities were nightly being indulged in by both sides in the House, we went one evening to hear a " debate." The regular business seemed to be conducted as well as it is at Westminster, but it was curious to see the careless way in which the members, in brown holland or yellow silk coats, lay about on the sofas, or lazily lounged off to the table for frequent draughts of what was said to be iced water. The shouts, cries, and interruptions were very unseemly, much worse than anything we had then experienced, giving us a very low opinion of the representatives of the people. One honourable member, in the course of debate, hurled a heavy tome across the house at the head of one of his opponents with crushing effect, while another member characterised the smile of the Minister of Lands as being such as to " sour all the milk in the colony, and to take the varnish off all the mahogany in the house." This compliment the Minister lightly parried by remarking that anything coming from the son of a cabbage hawker could not affect him.

The Melbourne legislators evidently do not believe in having "all work and no play," they have consequently provided themselves—of course out of the public purse—with billiard tables, and, with a spirit of rare generosity and thoughtfulness, have made the parliamentary reporters for the Press free of the rooms.

With such provision for their comfort, and with handsome salaries paid them for their services by a grateful country, what wonder that there should be considerable competition for seats within the walls of the Victorian House of Parliament? and with what feelings of commiseration must they regard their brethren of New South Wales, who, when one of their number recently proposed to imitate the example of Melbourne in the matter of billiard tables, were reminded, in unmistakable terms by their exacting constituents, that they were sent to Parliament to *work* and not to play! And what makes the matter harder for the Sydney legislators is the fact that, unlike their Melbourne friends, they are not paid for their services.

The question of the payment of Members of Parliament has acquired considerable interest in England of late, mainly in consequence of Mr. Chamberlain's declaration in its favour; and it appears not unlikely that at no distant date it may be carried into effect. There are two modes by which the object in view may be attained;—either by a general charge upon the Imperial Revenue, or by each constituency paying its own representative; in either case the amount of salary would be determined by Parliament; and, if the latter course be adopted, its payment would be made obligatory. In Victoria the salaries are paid direct from the Treasury, and those who have seen how the system works are the least enthusiastic in its favour.

Time was, when to be a Member of Parliament was looked upon as a certain way to repair a broken fortune, or to make a new one; but since the days when George III., of pious memory, taught his Ministers how to corrupt the Parliament, a seat in that assembly has not been considered to be pecuniarily advantageous. But in some of the Australian colonies the case is different, politics being looked upon, to a great extent, as a trade or profession, and very largely because of the salary attached to the position of Members of the Legislature.

One of my customers in Victoria, who had long owed me £50, told me he would soon be able to discharge his debt as he had been nominated for Parliament, and would pay me out of his first quarter's salary! It is only fair to say that, although he failed to secure the seat, he nevertheless paid his debt.

The Houses of Parliament stand on a slight elevation, and though still unfinished, promise to be a magnificent pile of buildings, of which many an old-established country, with far greater pretensions than Victoria, might well be proud. The Great Hall, a sort of ante-chamber to the Houses, impressed me as much as any building of the kind I had ever seen. It is about 180ft. long, by 60ft. wide, and 60ft. high, without galleries, seats, or anything to detract from its magnificent proportions. The whole surface of the walls and roof is covered with a beautiful enamel-like cement, brilliantly white and polished quite smooth, the floor being of white marble, and a superb white marble statue of the Queen in the centre. The whole effect is startlingly beautiful. I subsequently went over the Town Hall and Council Chamber, but these are much inferior to corresponding buildings in Birmingham. The councillors wear cocked hats and gold-braided coats, and the aldermen black stuff gowns or robes.

I have already spoken of the tension in party politics at the time of our visit. This was seized upon by the theatrical people, who produced an adaptation of the burlesque known in England as "Happy Land," the principal characters being Mr. Berry—the Premier, the man with the caustic smile, and another prominent member of the Administration. On the morning of the day on which the first representation was to have been given, a Cabinet Council was hastily summoned, and the question gravely debated as to whether the safety of the State, or at any rate the Cabinet, would not be compromised by tolerating the performance. It was quickly and unanimously decided to prohibit it, and this decision was announced. Such a universal storm of ridicule was thus aroused that the infatuated Berryites were driven to reconsider their course, ultimately licensing an emasculated version of the play, with all the political references erased. The newspapers, ever alive to the chance of turning a penny, and showing up an opponent, published the original *in extenso*, and when the performance began large numbers of the audience had copies before them.

When an excised passage was reached, the actor or actress would pause, and, holding up the hand, whisper audibly, "Hush! prohibited," giving time for those with copies to read the obnoxious reference. For days after people in the street would, on meeting, put up the finger, and greet each other with "Hush! prohibited." The Government were overwhelmed with ridicule, and were glad to compromise with the persons they had so injudiciously provoked.

During the summer Melbourne is occasionally visited by what are called "hot winds." They blow from the north, and derive much of their arid character from coming over the great wastes of the interior. We were unlucky enough to experience one of these hot winds, and we subsequently learned that the shade temperature had reached 117°—as high a point, I believe, as any that had previously been recorded in the city. It is no exaggeration to say that while exposed to the wind it felt like the hot blast from the cupola of a foundry when iron is being melted. The clothes were little or no protection against its scorching influence. The air was filled with choking clouds of dust, which penetrated everything and everywhere. In the evening, however, the wind fell off, leaving the temperature very high.

The sanitary arrangements in Melbourne are extremely defective, and to my mind fully justify the writer of the article on the "Black Death," which so much startled us on our arrival there. There is literally no system of sewerage, the whole drainage of the town running by the side of the pathways in wide ill-paved channels, crossed by wooden foot bridges. The whole runs into the river Yarra. In heavy rains these channels become surcharged, and the lower-lying streets are flooded with diluted sewage. On such an occasion I was crossing one of these gutters, when a street-sweeper approached, holding his cap in one hand and his broom in the other, and asked me to remember "an old shipmate, your honour." I soon recognised him as our old friend "Tall and Fat." I could not help looking surprised, whereat he assured me he had found a most excellent berth as a street-sweeper—that none but gentlemen were engaged in the "profession," all being Oxford or Cambridge men—the wages being 7s. per day. I asked after his friend "Short and Stout." He said he held a similar appointment at an adjoining corner, and he promised to share my gratuity with him.

The country between Melbourne and Ballarat is flat and somewhat uninteresting, but near the latter city it becomes more hilly and diversified. Ballarat is a well-built city, containing about 40,000 inhabitants. A few years ago there were 10,000 more, but in consequence of the alluvial gold becoming exhausted a considerable exodus took place. The streets are wide, and have trees on each side; in some there are trees in the middle as well. The houses are substantially built of stone or brick, and altogether it has the air of being a busy and prosperous place.

We visited one of the gold mines, and as we approached the office saw three persons coming towards it, one of them carrying a parcel, which appeared to be heavy. It proved to be a brick of gold weighing 33lbs., and worth about £1,200, being the result of one week's working. We were shown the various processes of obtaining the gold from the quartz, and were rather surprised at the somewhat primitive character of the machinery employed.

Gold Mine, Ballarat.

Several of the companies with big-sounding names occupy spaces of only 60ft. by 50ft., and yet yield substantial returns. One such little patch is part of the Church land, and is called "Hallelujah Claim," in honour of the Church. The total value of gold raised in Australia up to end of 1879 was 275 millions sterling.

One of the prettiest features of this handsome city is a fine sheet of water called Lake Wendouree. This lake is about a mile across, and lies in the crater of an extinct volcano. The Botanical Gardens are on the farther side of Wendouree, which has a fine boulevard round each side leading thereto. On the lake are

several pretty little steamers, which make frequent
excursions. In the evening they are provided with
coloured lamps, and music and dances may be enjoyed
by the passengers. Ballarat is less than thirty years
old, yet has quite an old-world appearance. It is a
charming city and well worth a visit, and we were well
pleased to have seen it.

A favourite excursion from Melbourne is to
the Black Spur Mountains, about two days' drive
from the city. Leaving Melbourne the route passes
through some miles of suburban villa residences with
beautiful gardens. After about ten miles "the bush"
is reached, and continues for the remainder of the
journey, relieved here and there by a clearing or by a
little village. The term "bush" must not be understood as scrub, furze, etc., but all kinds of uncultivated
land, thick forests, and open country. A curious feature
of colonial life is to see in full operation the old stage
coaches, so long ago discarded in England. They are
painted a brilliant red, and indeed appear to be the
veritable machines used in the "good old days when
George the Third was king." They are frequently drawn
by six or more horses, and, true to their ancient tradi-
tions, now and then have a spill, for roadmakers in the
Colonies have the same habit as their English brethren
of making short "right about turns" at the bottom
of steep hills. We drew up at a small wayside inn,
intending to bait the horses, but found it was closed,
owing to the death of the landlord. This man was a
large wine grower, and his vineyards extended for a
considerable distance round his house. After passing
through many miles of country under vine cultivation we

pulled up for the night at a little village called Healesville, where a very miscellaneous company sat down to a substantial repast, ending with what the waiter called a " soafler." The light being dim it was difficult to see what the dish really was, and curiosity being awakened, inquiry elicited the fact that it was intended for a *soufflé*. The hotel being quite full of visitors, two of our party had to sleep in the parlour on sofas of the horse-hair order. The landlord, coming in to see if we were all right, informed us we could not have our boots cleaned in the morning, as his man was just then out on a boose. A colonial friend travelling with us remarked that it was "awkward when master or man took to boosing." Our friend had previously told us that the landlord was generally "on that line." "You never saw me boosy!" said he. "*Never!*" retorted our friend, with peculiar emphasis, which summarily stopped the discussion. We were awakened early in the morning by the screams of laughing jackasses and the crowing of cocks. Our toilette was performed somewhat under difficulties, one of us having to use the piano as a washstand, and another being constrained to go through the same operation in the open street under the hotel verandah. Our route now lay over a steep hill, through a forest of gum trees, the fragrance arising from the latter in the early morning air being delightfully refreshing. The main roads are kept very fairly, a certain number of men being told off for each section at 9s. per day wages. The old corduroy roads, formed by laying trees across the track and filling the interstices with earth, are being gradually superseded by Macadam. The men seemed to work in very leisurely fashion. We were to have breakfasted at a cottage on the road, but when we arrived there found that the old lady who kept it had gone to a ball at some village public-house, several miles away, as also had the owners of all the other cottages along the route. A little girl left in charge told us that after the ball all these good people were going to the funeral of the wine grower and innkeeper previously mentioned, and our friend told us they would doubtless stay there to comfort the widow as long as there was any wine left in the house. We soon after entered the region of the big gum trees and of the tree ferns, and a wonderfully beautiful sight it was.

A Big Tree.

The whole valley is filled with tree ferns, and the fronds, in many cases being new, with the sunlight falling upon them, formed a picture not soon to be forgotten.

Some of the gum trees were enormously large—we saw several 15ft. in diameter and over 200ft. in height—but these were small when compared with some found in the less frequented parts. In the midst of such surroundings lies the pretty little village of Fernshaw. When we were first invited to spend a week at the country house of our friend we rather unreasonably pictured in our minds an English country or seaside residence, and anticipated much pleasure in the change from dusty Melbourne. Our surprise was great, therefore, when after jolting over some half-formed roads we came upon a clearing among the gum trees, and were told that the wooden shanty before us was the Melbourne citizen's country house. We were not disposed, however, to be very critical, for the sixty miles drive in the mountain air had made us hungry, and we were quite ready to respond to the invitation to the evening meal. But our dis-illusion was complete upon entering the sitting room and finding that no provision had been made for the satisfying of our keen appetites. By some accident the supplies from Melbourne had not arrived; the rough table was covered with a couple of towels, and on it was spread a repast consisting of some bad bread and sour raspberry jam, while the "cup which cheers but not inebriates" was innocent of milk and sugar. It was Saturday evening and we were "out of humanity's reach," being many miles from any source of supply, so had to content ourselves as best we might with this Spartan fare until the Monday, when our host proposed an excursion to a distant part, involving the staying a night at an hotel. We gladly embraced the proposal, and finding that the hotel was a comfortable one I determined to excuse myself from joining in the excursion on the following day in order that I might have the opportunity of recruiting nature's exhausted powers by an extra meal, a resolution I had much satisfaction in carrying into effect. Our friend and his sons own about one thousand acres, at present covered with trees, with the exception of a small clearing round the house. When a piece of land is taken, the first care is to fence it, which is done with logs, at a cost of £25 per mile, including the cutting of the logs. The next step is to "ring" the trees—that is, to cut a deep groove round them, and so by killing them prevent any further exhaustion of the soil. The trees being dead, vegetation rapidly springs up, and there is soon abundance of food for cattle. Clearing the ground of trees and stumps is a very costly operation, and takes many years to finally accomplish. The Government with a view of preventing the accumulation of lands in a few hands, refuse to sell more than 320 acres to one person, but of course this is easily evaded. At the time of our visit the price was £1 per acre, payable in ten years by equal instalments, a condition being that some one should reside upon the allotment. At the end of three years the owner can obtain from Government a lease of the land, and can then pay up the full value, which leaves him at liberty to sell if he wishes to do so. Of course the building up of large estates is thus encouraged, but this could, perhaps, be prevented by imposing a tax on every acre. The 20,000 acre men would soon be compelled to dispose of some of the land which they hold in the expectation that it will

On the Black Spur.

increase in value. Such a plan has been proposed, but it naturally met with great opposition from the landed interest.

Leaving our friend's house a drive of a few miles through the bush brought us to the picturesquely-situated village of Marysville. This little village lies in a deep hollow surrounded by fine ranges of tree-clad hills of extreme beauty. A pleasant hour's walk from the village, under the shade of the tree ferns, took us to the Stephenson Falls. The principal fall is 80ft., and the volume of water is unusually large for an Australian waterfall. Close to the fall are some magnificently large tree ferns, and while sitting here enjoying the lovely view some little birds came flitting about, one of them hopping on to the shoulder of one of our party, attracted, doubtless, by the aroma of a fragrant " weed " which at the time he was enjoying. English visitors to Australia, especially those in search of health, would find the conditions existing at Marysville most conducive to their restoration. The air is bracing, and as before stated, the scenery most delightful. A tolerably good accommodation is to be had at the inn, which will doubtless be improved as the place becomes more widely known.

Returning to Melbourne, we stayed another night at Healesville, arriving at 7.30, and as we had fared badly during the day we were quite ready for a substantial dinner, and from our previous experience of the house made no doubt of obtaining it. But unfortunately for us, there had been a chapel tea-party during the afternoon, at which a large force of parsons had been present. We had therefore to be content with a tough,

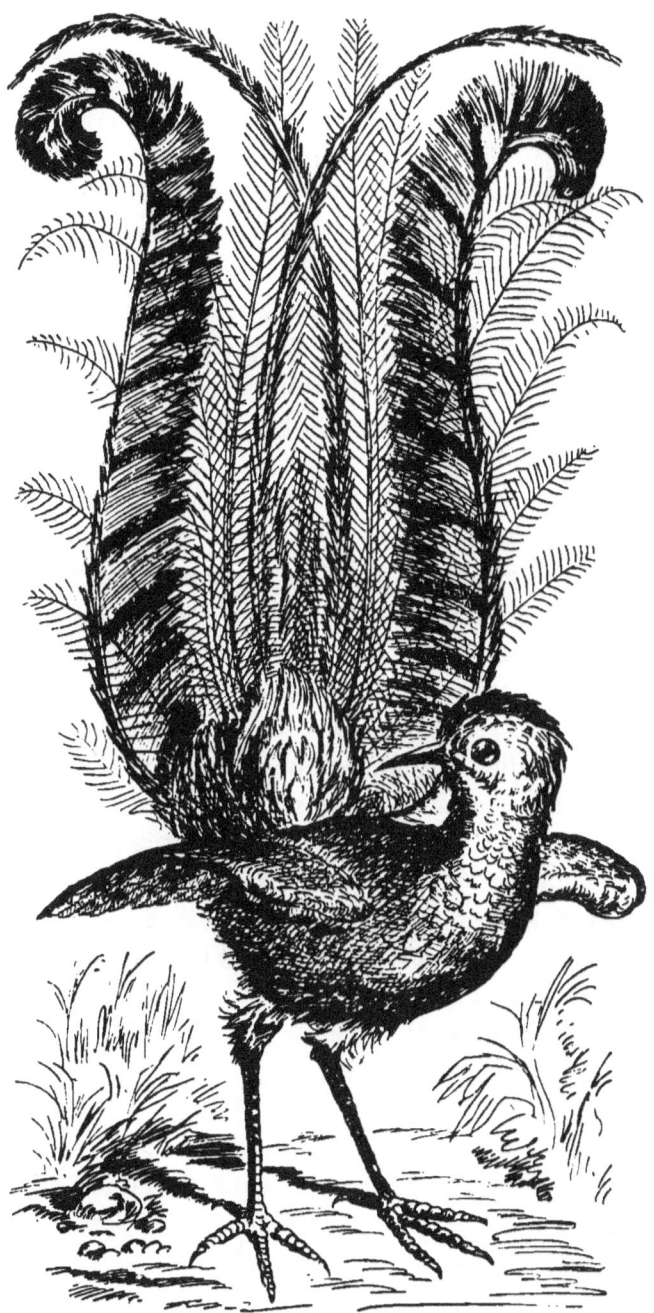

THE LYRE BIRD.

woody steak, a wild duck of ancient and fish-like smell, varied by salted mutton. The butter was rancid and full of dead flies, and the bread appeared to have been cast upon the waters. We had to go to bed feeling quite faint, but hoping for a better breakfast. The beds were good, and we should have had a good night's rest, which we sorely needed after the twig beds of the previous night at the Marysville Hotel, but the partitions between the rooms being only of half-inch plank everything passing around us could be heard all too plainly. A little after midnight some fellows came in from night-fishing, and going into the room next ours woke us up by a great noise. One old donkey was telling the two younger ones he had had a deal of experience among snakes, killing as many as eight a day for many years, and that as the result of a series of experiments during that time he had found an infallible cure for snake bites. He had offered his discovery to the Government for £1,000, and his partner offered to be poisoned by the most deadly snakes to test its efficacy, but all to no purpose. So he had determined to let the secret die with him. The others asked if the sovereign remedy was to be swallowed. "Oh, no," said the old fellow, "for it is composed of five deadly poisons." "You must first cut out the wounded part, and rub the antidote in." "But," added he, "the secret shall now die with me." "But how about your partner?" asked the others. "Won't he tell the secret?" "Oh no," was the reply; "he's safe enough, for he's dead." Then we heard the voice of the landlord's pretty daughter telling them it was time to go to sleep, upon which the old boy growled,

"I wonder people can't go to sleep without bothering me." The rest of the night was made miserable for us by the two "night fishers," who, rising long before dawn, went prowling about the different rooms, ours included, collecting their tackle for a shooting expedition, but leaving behind them, as we found afterwards, their percussion caps.

We returned to Melbourne by another route, affording us some fine views of the plains called Yarra Flats, and the Marysville Hills in the far distance.

COLLINS STREET.

CHAPTER IV.

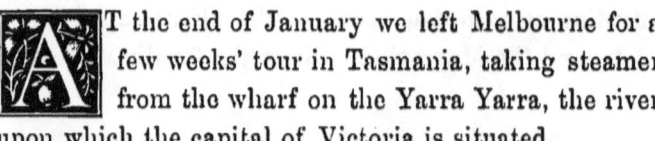 T the end of January we left Melbourne for a few weeks' tour in Tasmania, taking steamer from the wharf on the Yarra Yarra, the river upon which the capital of Victoria is situated.

The banks of the Yarra have been selected as the scene of the operations of all the most offensive trades in the colony—the bone boilers, tanners, fellmongers, candle makers, chemical manure makers, glue manufacturers. In addition to the abominations proceeding from these factories, all the sewage which is not left on the surface of the streets is run into the stream. The river is very narrow, the fall to the sea extremely slight, and the traffic great, hence at every revolution of the paddle-wheel or screw-propeller the abominations from the depths below are stirred up and mingled with those coming from the before-named savoury factories, forming a more horrible compound than ever proceeded from witches' cauldron. In this one respect the New World has certainly shot far ahead of the old, for even the memory of ancient Cologne is made savoury to the nostrils by this colonial stench.

Our friends came to say good-bye, and brought quite a sack of peaches and apricots, which were very acceptable during the voyage. If there were on board any roysterers or betting men they had no opportunity for displaying their peculiarities. Until we reached the entrance to the river Tamar almost every person on board was ill, for Bass's Straits is notorious for its disagreeable cross seas.

Launceston is forty miles up the river, and is the capital of the county of Cornwall, as in England. The scenery along the river banks is very beautiful, and is so exactly like the Truro river at home that it is difficult to believe we are out of England. The river is winding and broad, and the shores slope gently down from high ground covered with trees. Here and there are bright green meadows and villages and scattered farmsteads and churches. I saw nothing in Victoria to compare with it.

Launceston, a quiet city of 10,000 inhabitants, is surrounded by hills. Looking down upon it, one is reminded of Florence from Fiesole, the beautiful climate and clear air being quite Italian, with the lovely Tamar winding its circuitous route for miles away. We drove out towards a place called the "Devil's Punch Bowl," walking the last mile through a beautiful wood down a hill, with firs, gum trees, etc., in abundance, with here and there delightful glimpses of green glades. The air was filled with the sounds of the tree locusts and the tremendous hissing noise of the *cicadas*, the sun shining through the trees and producing a temperature and light which were simply perfect. The only drawback is the presence of snakes, which, our driver said, are very abundant here. The scene is truly English. At the bottom of the little wooded valley we came upon an old wooden shanty, where we tried to get a glass of milk, but there was no one at home. Presently an old man appeared, driving cows. We asked him for milk—he had none, but gave us water, and offered raw eggs. My companion took two, and said he liked them, but I am sure he liked the first best. The old man was seventy-three years of age, and lived there alone, sleeping on a door covered with an opossum rug. He told us his master died there close by the bee-hives a few weeks ago, " so, said he, " I put the bees in deep mourning, or they would all have left."

I wrote my notes sitting on a gatepost, out of the way of snakes; the moon shone brightly, and in the distance I could hear the church bells, mingled with the voices of children, the tinkling of cowbells, and barking of dogs.

The shops close at six o'clock, but the public-houses of course remain open. I observed a small fruit-shop, a mere shanty, with the sign of " Pomona's Temple," and a hairdresser's saloon with the high-sounding name of " Tonsorial Palace," while a democratic opponent in the same street, with a proud humility, called his place of business a " Barber's Shop."

Strolling in the town one evening I talked with a policeman, who was an almost exact counterpart of Count Moltke. He had just received his new regulation helmet, and did not like it at all: it was hard and heavy. He was very pleased to hear we liked Tasmania better than Victoria. "Ah," said he, "you will find real hospitality here; here everybody helps everybody, but in Melbourne everybody helps himself, and the bobby or somebody catches the hindmost." He said he had been a policeman for twenty years, and, "although I say it as shouldn't, I will say for the Launceston police, they are the most civillest, honestest body of policemen going," with which I quite agreed.

Another beautiful ride is to the Cora Linn, seven miles from Launceston. On one side of the road, stretching almost the whole distance, is a hedge of sweetbriar, giving forth delicious perfume. It is difficult to get accustomed to the reversal of the seasons; here in February the farmers are busy cutting and saving their corn, but with no fear of rain to spoil their harvest, as in England. A bridge crosses the Linn, and a cataract-like stream tumbles down over rocks, very much like the Lynn at Lynmouth. Below the bridge is a deep basin, and all around are numbers of queer trees, young and old, with many burnt-out trunks black as negroes, with white spots in them like eyes. The trees and shrubs are full of *cicadas* making a great noise.

Leaving Launceston, we drove to Falmouth, ninety miles away. The road lies through a beautifully-wooded country; indeed, the entire ride is just like going through a park in England. We saw lots of magpies, very much larger than ours, but quite as mischievous. A gentleman told us a person once asked him to change a sovereign, which he did, and then looked for the sovereign, but it could not be seen. Presently, looking up, he saw Master Mag in a shrub, with one eye shut, his head on one side, and standing on one leg, with the piece of gold in his mouth.

Our first night's stopping-place was at Stoney Creek, where there is a comfortable hotel, just like a private house, with only one other house for miles around. Near to the hotel flows the River Esk, a black, silent, swiftly-flowing and suicidal-looking stream, suggestive in its motion of some huge black snake, of which there are many in the neighbourhood. In crossing a field to look at the river our clothes became covered with burrs and spines from the prickly pear. We sat down on a grassy mound to watch the flowing of the river, but had quickly to move, as we found ourselves in the midst of a colony of great ants. The following verses were written on the occasion by one of my companions:

The Doctor Contemplates—A Poem.
(From a sketch by the Author).

THOU AND I.

Thou art in happy England
 With peace, content, and joy,
And there no poisonous reptiles
 Thy comfort can destroy;
No hissing sound the startled ear
 With fear of death awakes—
Thou art in happy England,
 I, in the land of snakes.

About thy household duties
 Serenely thou canst go,
No fear of fierce tarantulas
 Or scorpion brings thee woe;
And day by day flows calmly on,
 And sleep wings through the night—
Thou art in happy England,
 I, where mosquitos bite.

Thou hast the trusty faithful dog,
 The quiet, harmless cat,
But I the fierce Tasmanian D——,
 Opossum, and wombat;
Familiar objects greet thy sight,
 Here all is strange and new—
Thou art in happy England,
 I, with the kangaroo.

Thou hast the blithe canary,
 The robin chirps to thee,
While here the magpies chatter
 And rail from every tree;
Bright parrots glint beneath the sun,
 And shriek their hideous song—
Thou art in happy England,
 I, wattle-birds among.

Thou canst recline in any place,
 And watch the moments pass,
Here burrs and prickles fill the clothes
 While lying on the grass,
They stick into the flesh, and sting
 Like gnat, or wasp, or bee—
But thou in happy England
 From all such plagues art free.

> Hurrah for happy England,
>   For all the folk at home!
> From hill and dale resounds the cry,
>   No matter where we roam.
> Rare scenes of beauty greet the sight,
>   The balmy air is sweet,
> But still I sigh for England
>   Where thou and I shall meet.
>
> Dr. L——.

The landlady was a widow, her husband having recently died. Her son had just returned from sea, where he had been for twelve years. He had been wrecked three times, and the last time should have given him enough of the sea for the rest of his life. It was in the ship "Euxine," taking 3,000 tons of coal to the Mauritius. She took fire off the Cape of Good Hope in the midst of a terrific storm. The captain was washed overboard and drowned; a sailor was also swept away, and while only twenty feet from the ship was attacked by a flock of albatrosses, right in sight of his comrades. He fought with them, but all in vain, and the wretches literally pulled him in pieces with their strong bills in a very few minutes. The crew got out the boats, but of course they were in a bad state. It was, however, a choice between burning and drowning, so they put off, preferring to risk the latter. After two or three days, two of the boats were picked up, but the third was out for eleven days. The poor wretches on board had nothing whatever to eat, and in their extremity were driven to cast lots which among them should die. One unhappy man was disposed of, and in two hours after a ship came in sight and picked them up.

"SWEET VALE OF AVOCA." 67

A lovely drive through Epping Forest brought us to Avoca, where " the bright waters meet," the North and South Esk uniting here. Our route lay along a fine road, through avenues of gum trees, wattles (acacias), cultivated for their bark, the sweetbriars and hawthorns scenting the air delightfully. We saw a splendid eagle, and large numbers of parrots, magpies, and hawks.

AVOCA (from a sketch by J. Willis).

On our way we passed many residences of great wool-growers, owning as much as 20,000 acres of land each, but living, for the most part, in England, their affairs in the Colony being managed by agents. They keep only one man on each 5,000 acres. There is scarcely any agriculture, although the land is very suitable, but being taken up in this way, there is no room for population to increase, and the people have to emigrate.

At Fingal we stopped at an hotel, kept by an Irishman married to a Jewess. They presided at either end of the table, and kept us short of food; indeed, I never saw a small joint go so far before. Next day we left the hotel, still hungry, although the charges were quite as high as those at the Great Western Hotel, Paddington.

Soon after leaving Fingal we saw something by the roadside which looked very like a snake, and on examining it we found it was one—a black snake, 4ft. 6in. long. It lay perfectly still, and presently we found it was dead; but the sensation was not pleasant. A gentleman at the hotel told us he had killed four the night previously, and doubtless this was one of them.

St. Mary's (from a sketch by the Author).

After passing through the charming village of St. Mary's, embowered in trees, we entered a lovely avenue, two miles in length, filled with beautiful flowers and ferns, the air laden with scents from the gum and other trees, and on emerging came upon St. Mary's Pass. This is an immense gorge, four miles long, filled with fine trees, the road, which is remarkably good, being cut in the side of the cliff by convicts in the old days of Van Diemen's Land. It winds down the valley to the sea at Falmouth, and on either side rise lofty hills, while the valley below is 1,000 feet deep, and filled with immense trees of various kinds, including the tree fern. I have seen most of the passes and valleys in the Tyrol, but have never seen one to excel this in grandeur or beauty.

FALMOUTH HOTEL (from a sketch by J. Willis).

In the map the word "Falmouth" was printed in rather large letters, so we expected to find a somewhat considerable place. At the head of the pass we were told the township lay between the foot of the hill and the sea. On getting down the hill we could plainly view the sea and the intervening land, but no town was visible. Inquiring of some little boys the way to Falmouth, they directed us away to the right. We went on, feeling assured we were going wrong; and presently, meeting a gentleman, we inquired again, when he told us to retrace our course, to go through an ordinary field gate, and that we should then get to Falmouth in three minutes! We told him that the little boys had directed us the other way, but he said we should have asked for "Hotel." The town of Falmouth, where the boys lived, consisted of two or three houses, and was a mile from the hotel. On exploring the place next day we were informed that fifty years before it was much more important than now. Miles of streets were marked out, but were grass-grown, and there were not more than a dozen houses in the place, all built of wood,

BURIAL-PLACE AT FALMOUTH (from a sketch by the Author).

and of one storey in height. The burying-place for the district is about a mile away, on the open common, each grave being surrounded with stakes, with no wall or fence enclosing the whole. It was a melancholy sight, reminding me strongly of the graves on the battle-fields of the Franco-German war.

The beach and sands are very fine, like those of my native county. The bathing is delightful, but you must keep a sharp look out for sharks. One morning, however, while bathing, we stood in much greater danger from the mad folly of some Cockneys who had recently come to the hotel. We had been bathing in an arm of the sea, the point beyond which it was not safe being marked by a stake driven into the sand. Between our bathing place and the hotel was a high sand bank, screening us from sight, the stake being visible from the verandah of the hotel. After dressing, we were leisurely walking up the sandbank towards the hotel, when we were startled by a bullet passing between our heads and lodging in the sand behind us! We threw up our towels and shouted, and then saw the Cockney sportsman standing on the platform under the verandah, from whence he had been aiming at the stake in the sand with his rifle for the past half hour. On examination we found the sand riddled with bullets, not 50ft. from where we had been bathing. The little burying ground possessed a new significance in our eyes after this incident. We found some beautiful sea-shells during a delightful walk along the beach towards Swansea, and on our return called upon the gentleman who put us right for Falmouth on our arrival. He is a farmer from near Oxford, and had been here seven or eight years, finding it a terribly lonely place. Recently his nine children and his servants took the measles, and his wife being ill, he had to nurse them all. When they got well his wife sickened and died, leaving him with seven daughters and two sons, the eldest being only fourteen years old. The nearest doctor lived more than thirty miles away.

In order to get to Hobart Town, we had to retrace our steps some sixty miles, as there is only one road on this side of the island. We stayed a night at Avoca, a charming place, but the roads were a foot deep in dust. Although the climate is so fine, and everything favours the growth of fruit, there is very little grown. It is alleged that fruit trees do not prosper, but I had ample evidence that the cause is to be found in the indifference or laziness of the people. Strolling in the neighbourhood of the village, we came upon a beautiful orchard, and were admiring the large, ripe plums, when a voice behind said, " Walk in, gentlemen, and help yourselves." The speaker was a hearty old man, who had lived here forty-six years. He came from Ledbury, and was much interested in hearing about Birmingham. He told us that the day before he left England he walked from Ledbury to Birmingham to see the Nelson statue in the Bull Ring.

The old man told us a snake story, which strikingly illustrates the vitality of these reptiles. A short time previously he and his son went across a neighbouring mountain on horseback to visit one of their farms. Going " single file " between the trees, the son, who was leading, suddenly called out to his father, " Look out, there's a snake," and at the same instant his horse started. The old gentleman got off, and finding it was a black snake,—one of the most venomous species— caught up a stick, and aimed a blow at it. The stick however was rotten, and broke without hurting the reptile, which now prepared to strike; but the old man managed to get his heel upon its head, and ground it into the earth; and having, as he thought, killed it, tied a piece of string around its middle, and bending a wattle tree down, attached the end of the string to one of the branches, and then released the tree. They thought no more of the matter until three days after, when two of his men, returning from his farm with a cart, were seen by their master dragging a snake behind the cart. He asked them where they caught it; they explained that while coming down the hill side, their attention was arrested by a snake in a tree dashing towards them, but unable to release itself. On examination, they found it was tied up! "So that after all," said the old man, "it was only scotched, not killed."

A fellow-traveller on the coach told us that he was coming from the tin mines near Mount Bischoff, and that for some months he and his partner had slept in hammocks slung from trees. One night, just as he was going to sleep, something dropped from the tree across his body. He took it in his hand, and finding it was a snake, he flung it from him, when it alighted on his companion. Luckily, both escaped unhurt. He also told me of the experience of a friend of his, a Government surveyor, who was frequently in the woods for weeks together, with one or two men. This gentleman slept in a hammock suspended from trees. The hammock was in reality a sack, hanging some feet from the ground, into which he got at night. One night he had retired as usual, and being very wearied, did not at once notice that there was independent movement at his feet. Very soon, however, he realised the fact that a snake had gone to bed before him, and was coiling itself round his legs. The gentleman quickly got out, unhurt, and soon killed the snake.

I also read in a colonial paper another account of a night adventure with a snake. A lady had retired to rest, and was fast asleep; the weather being very hot, one of her arms was outside the clothes, and during the night she was awakened by feeling something trying to force its way between her arm and her side; she quickly realised the situation, and without moving, tightly pressed her arm against her body and prevented the venomous reptile from getting between, when presently it glided over her shoulder and fell on the floor with a thud. She was soon out of bed at the other end, and calling for help and a light the snake was quickly despatched.

The doctor in this place has charge of a district sixty miles in diameter, and always expects his fees before leaving his house; but although he has so large a district, I question if he makes his fortune, for although acres are many, people are few, and the salubrity of the climate does not favour the medical profession.

The main road between Launceston and Hobart is struck at Willis's Corner, a few miles from Campbelltown—the principal town in the interior of the island. There is a station here on the main-line railway. The gauge of the line is thirty-nine inches, I think.

Campbelltown is a straggling place, with streets enough laid out for a city, but with only few houses, and it is not likely many more will be built, as the railway is expected to take away its trade, which depends mainly upon the coach traffic. The streets are about one hundred and twenty feet wide, which is greatly in excess of all requirements, and causes the traffic to run in ruts, instead of being distributed over the roadway, giving a desolate appearance to the whole place. As a rule, the Tasmanian roads are very good, having been made in the old days by convict labour, but you must not venture to mention the word "convict;" the people all speak of these public works as having been executed by Government. Having had so much done for them by the Government, the Tasmanian people are lacking in energy, and are much too prone to rely upon outside help; and yet when Melbourne people come over to invest capital in mines and other industries, the cry is that the strangers are taking all the money out of the country. As I have said, the farms are of a great size, but the number of men engaged are but few. The farmers have two great enemies—the thistle and the rabbit. It is said the former was introduced into the colonies by a patriotic Scotchman, to remind him of his bonnie Scotland, the rabbit being introduced for the purpose of sport; but, like our old friend the sparrow, they have so increased as to be the cause of serious loss, and are the subjects of special legislation. Some landowners spend many thousands of pounds in putting walls around their estates to keep the rabbits out.

From Campbelltown to Hobart is seventy-six miles, and we rode the whole distance in a single day. The country is very beautiful, and towards the end of the journey we had fine mountain and river scenery. The Derwent is a splendid river, running through a lovely country, sometimes through rich pasture lands and hop gardens, and at other times between high precipices and rugged country.

Mount Wellington is a remarkably fine mountain of 4,000 feet in height, and is topped with snow for a considerable portion of the winter.

SUMMIT OF MOUNT WELLINGTON.

Villages are very scarce on the road, and shops few, so the inhabitants get most of their requirements from hawkers, who visit all parts of the island with horses and vans, carrying all kinds of goods. We passed several with their wares spread out on the ground. Our coachman told us rather a good story of two of these "merchants," as they are usually called. These men travelled the road together as partners, having a standing agreement between them that only one should get drunk at a time, so that they were not unfrequently seen riding, one of them as drunk as a lord or a fiddler, while the other was perfectly sober, but merry. One day, however, they broke the rule, and both got drunk together, letting their horse go just as it liked. Unhappily, as they were turning a corner in the road, a coach came bowling along and ran into them, breaking their van and many of their bones, besides spoiling most of their stock-in-trade. The coachman could not tell us if the accident had the effect of making the men teetotallers.

VIEW IN THE PUBLIC GARDENS, HOBART.

Hobart (as Hobart Town is now called) is most beautifully situated, with extensive public gardens, charmingly laid out, and having the advantage of an abundance of water from the River Derwent. The Governor's house is admirably placed, commanding extensive views of river and mountain scenery. The citizens are exceedingly hospitable, and we were not long at the hotel before we were visited by a gentleman who informed us he had entered our names on the books of the principal club, and also invited us to a grand representation of " Martha." There are many charming excursions in the neighbourhood of Hobart. One of the most beautiful is to New Norfolk, about two and a half hours' steam up the Derwent river. As we approach New Norfolk the river gets very narrow, and we pass through a part called "Hell Gates," having steep lofty cliffs on one side, and a beautiful tongue of land with trees and lovely green grass on the other. The name I thought particularly ill chosen.

The village of New Norfolk is prettily situated among the hills, with the lovely Derwentwater at its feet. Its principal industry is the growing of hops. We went into the gardens, and saw the people busily picking the hops, which were very fine.

Another beautiful excursion is to Fern Tree Valley, a lovely spot with a fine avenue of tree ferns, and with many immense gum trees in the surrounding woods.

There being no steamer to Sydney or Melbourne for a week, we drove over the road to Launceston, 120 miles distant. Soon after leaving Hobart we crossed the River Jordan, passed through Jericho, near to Jerusalem, stopping at Bagdad for breakfast.

Although February had just gone, the weather was still intensely hot. The harvest was nearly over, and the wheat looked beautiful. I saw some eight feet high, and a person told me he had frequently seen it grow as high as ten feet. Lunching at Melton Mowbray, we came on to Oatlands, driving the last few miles by moonlight, the night being very cool.

At Oatlands is a large gaol, where in old times a number of England's sons were confined, many of them having been sent there for political "offences," which in our happier times have conducted the best of Englishmen to the Council Board at Windsor. The gaol is now almost untenanted. In passing along we saw the ruins of many of the miserable old barracks, where the convicts used to live. Everything looks half finished, and I have scarcely seen one window blind furnished with cords for winding; they roll them up and pin them, consequently the blind is full of pin holes. We stopped a night at the best hotel in Campbelltown, a really well-appointed

OUR WAITER AT CAMPBELLTOWN (from a sketch by the Author).

house; but on trying to open the front door, the knob came off in my hand! We greatly enjoyed our three weeks' stay in Tasmania; in many respects it is more interesting than the mainland, while the climate is much more agreeable to Englishmen. A pleasant passage of twenty hours brought us to Melbourne again, and the weather being still very hot, we decided to go on to Sydney by steamer.

STARTING.

CHAPTER V.

THE run down Port Phillip Harbour to the Heads takes about four hours, and just inside the mouth of the harbour are two little watering-places, much frequented by the citizens of Melbourne.

Presently we come to a curious feature in the water. The currents of the bay and those of the open sea meet, and produce at their junction the phenomenon locally known as "The Rip." All at once, as the steamer comes out of the bay, we pass from smooth water into the regular waves of the sea; there is almost a wall between, and as the vessel passes through it a rushing sound is heard, the vessel instantly beginning to roll and pitch. In rough weather passing through "The Rip" is quite exciting, the water frequently rushing over the decks.

After a voyage of a little more than two days, we arrived outside the heads of Port Jackson or Sydney Harbour. Everyone has heard of the extreme beauty

SYDNEY HARBOUR.

of this glorious harbour; indeed if the visitor stays a few days in the city he is likely to hear of it many times. The entrance is about a mile in width, between bold cliffs 250 feet in height. It has a coast line of more than 250 miles, and is full of beautiful creeks and bays, with their banks finely wooded to the water's edge, and having numerous handsome villas picturesquely placed upon every point of vantage, the city being situated at the head of the bay. The old town of Sydney is very badly laid out, with narrow, crooked streets, while the pavements and roads are most execrable, and the drainage and water supply are as bad as they can well be. The public buildings, and the modern portion of the city, are very fine, the post-office in particular being a very handsome edifice, infinitely superior to the new post-office in Birmingham; but then the citizens of Sydney built their own, while the citizens of Birmingham were not consulted, and had to accept what the London architect was graciously pleased to bestow.

Next to the harbour, the public gardens of Sydney form its principal attraction. The Botanical Gardens are exceedingly fine, and contain a magnificent collection of almost every known tree that will stand the climate. A special feature is the Norfolk Island pine, which grows to a great height, perfectly straight, and with very regular branches. The gardens are finely situated on undulating ground, sloping down to the harbour, which is sufficiently deep 200 yards off to float men-of-war. From these gardens a fine view of the Governor's house and of other parts of the city is obtained. There is also a beautiful view from the Observatory Hill, which the Sydney people are justly proud of, for it can scarcely be equalled in any other part of the world. The harbour, with its numerous islands, lies spread out before the eyes, while the greatest animation is given to the scene by the large number of little steamers, yachts, and sail-boats continually flitting about, for the youth of Sydney are truly British in their love of the water. While we were admiring this panorama one morning, an old gentleman, observing we were strangers, pointed out the various objects of interest. Presently one of our party observing a strange cloud in the hitherto cloudless sky, called the old man's attention to it. At first he thought it was a bush fire away to the south, but in a minute he said, "Come on, we had better get under shelter, for it is a 'southerly buster!'"

A "southerly buster" is one of the institutions of Sydney, and is a hurricane of wind which comes up suddenly from the south, bringing clouds of dust from the brickfields lying on that side of the city. We had long been wishing to see a genuine example, and here it was with a vengeance. In less time than it takes to describe, the whole city and harbour were completely obscured by a tremendous cloud of dust, blown on at a great pace, roaring like a furnace, and carrying before it sticks, paper, and even small gravel, which strike with the force of hailstones. During the twenty minutes which the hurricane lasts umbrellas are perfectly useless, and every person and thing becomes completely covered with dust. Having experienced the "buster" once, we have no desire for a repetition.

Sydney is fortunate in possessing almost inexhaustible supplies of oysters, and the old gentleman referred to above told us they sometimes grew on trees! There is a tree called the Mangrove, which grows very plentifully on the banks of the Parramatta river; sometimes the water is very high for days together, and the oyster spawn gets fixed in the mud on the branches, and so they grow and are gathered in their season.

One of the most delightful excursions from Sydney is to the top of the Blue Mountains, where there are several villages and some exceedingly fine and interesting scenery. The summit of the mountains is about 3,500ft. above sea-level, and is seventy miles from Sydney, being reached by a picturesque zigzag railway. In the old convict days it was commonly supposed by the prisoners that China lay on the other side of the Blue Mountain range, and many of the wretched men lost their lives in the jungle in trying to escape to the celestial country; one party succeeded in getting to a considerable distance before the guard overtook them, and one of them was found to have in his possession an engraving of a compass, by which he expected to steer his way!

The railway from Sydney passes many charming villages and extensive orange groves, crossing the River Nepean by a handsome iron bridge.

Some of the hotels on the mountain are of a very primitive character. One of those in which we stayed was a single-storied building, with bed-rooms opening into the yard. The house was built of planks, and the partitions were not very thick. I found that the landlord was the brother of an English tradesman with whom I do business. They had not heard of one another

COTTAGE AT MOUNT VICTORIA.

for forty years, which was a suspicious circumstance, considering the history of the colony.

In the fireplace of our sitting room we found a "gin" set for rats, which during the night were quite lively. One morning we observed that our waiter seemed to be very anxious for us to finish our breakfast. Presently he asked if we had finished with the coffee-pot, saying that all the others had been sent to be mended, and as he had a rather particular couple in the next room, he did not like to take in the coffee in a tea-pot!

At Mount Victoria, the highest village on the mountain, there are good State schools, to which the children come for twenty-five miles round from the villages along the railway. Both schools and railways in New South Wales belong to the State, and the school-children are allowed to ride free by all trains. Even the goods trains have carriages attached for the use of the children, and the school hours are arranged to enable them to take advantage of the trains. Mount Victoria is a beautiful village, where many of the wealthy citizens of Sydney have charming residences. It has quite an alpine appearance with its wooden houses and tree-clad hills. In the neighbourhood are many delightful places, to which excursions are made; one of the most interesting is to a waterfall called "Govett's Leap." The road is a very rough one, and goes through the forest, in which are numbers of large ant-hills more than 5ft. in height, and formed of clay, which has become so hard that a stick makes no impression upon them. The entrances for the little creatures are very narrow cracks, too narrow for any of their enemies to get through. Sometimes, however, a creature called the "iguana" manages to make its way inside, when he always clears the entire colony out.

After a few miles' drive along an almost level road, we come suddenly upon the edge of a precipice nearly 1,000 feet deep, down which the stream falls forming

GOVETT'S LEAP, BLUE MOUNTAINS.

the waterfall. The "leap" is about 500 feet, and almost all the water becomes spray before it reaches the bottom, its appearance reminding us of the Staubbach Falls at Lauterbrunnen.

From the precipice a fine view is obtained for many miles round. The country is broken up into deep ravines or wide gullies, stretching as far as the eye can reach, and all wooded, while, except the little waterfall, not a drop of water is to be seen.

On the other side of Mount Victoria, towards Bathurst, is another curious zigzag railway, at the foot of which is the village of Lithgow, the seat of iron and coal industries. At present the works are of a very primitive character, but I have no doubt that at no distant date they will assume important proportions.

DESCENT TO HARTLEY VALE.

Outside our hotel door the landlord kept his talking parrot, which was always saying to the passers-by, "a bucket of beer, a bucket of beer." There was a retired missionary staying at the hotel with his wife, and one day the old lady told me that she thought they might have taught the poor thing something "more Christian."

One evening some drovers from Bathurst camped for the night near to the hotel; they put their cattle into a field, and having taken their tents from the pack-horses, soon made themselves comfortable round their camp-fires, the whole scene being very picturesque and gipsy-like.

This used to be the old coach-road before the railway was opened, and many a coach has been stopped and robbed by gangs of escaped convicts called bush-rangers. People were easily frightened in those days. A woman coming out of a cottage at night has been known to stop a coach, and snapping the spring of an old candlestick has ordered the passengers to "bail up" and to throw the mail-bags out, which being done under terror of the supposed pistol, she commanded them to drive on; the coachman of course supposing there was a gang of ruffians lying in wait.

Bushrangers are not yet a thing of the past, for while we were in Sydney four were sentenced to death for the murder of a policeman, who was one of a party sent in pursuit of the gang.

Hard by our hotel is a solitary graveyard, where lie the bodies of many convicts who died while confined in a neighbouring stockade in the old transportation days. A more desolate and melancholy place it would be impossible to imagine. Some of the public-houses have queer mottoes on their sign boards. We observed three not far apart having these inscriptions: "Labour in Vain," "The Leisure Hour," "The Rag and Famish." A favourite drink amongst the people is sarsaparilla, which is generally mentioned on the sign along with the beer.

Some of the birds in the woods about Mount Victoria make a great noise at night; one in particular, called the "Great Goat Sucker," is continually crying for "more pork," "more pork"; while another, the "Laughing Jackass" or "Great Kingfisher," greets the rising sun with his insane laughter. In the daytime he performs a very useful service by waging perpetual war against the snakes.

THE LAUGHING JACKASS.

The ants in Australia are rather formidable creatures. Some of them are more than an inch in length, and one kind, called the "bull-dog," is very fierce, and will attack anything; he can run backwards or forwards with equal facility, and never turns his back to the foe.

Their hills are very large, and a slight tap brings numbers of them out at once, and unless you want to be well punished, you had better leave them quickly, for their bite is something to be remembered. One morning while on a walk we observed two boys "prodding" an ant-hill; but by the time we had come up to them we found them otherwise engaged, for the "bull-dogs" had got up their clothes and were causing the boys to jump about as though they were "possessed;" occasionally they would pause and rub their legs with great devotion; and altogether it was apparent they felt their position keenly. As we passed them they gave us a ghastly smile, and I think they will let "sleeping bull-dogs lie" in the future.

THE AUTHOR SKETCHING (from a sketch by J. Willis).

During one of my visits to Sydney the political situation was this:—Two questions were before the Parliament and country—viz., an Amended Education Act, and an Excise Act, by which latter it was proposed to put a tax upon colonial beer.

"It happens that a vacancy has occurred in an important constituency, and as these questions are greatly agitating the whole country, the election is looked forward to with great interest as being a sort of test of the public sentiment. The Government candidate of course supports the two measures above referred to, while the opposition candidate is adverse to both, the latter being the largest brewer in the Colony (which of course accounts for his opposing the excise duty on beer), and, what is not unusual in the case of brewers, he is a decided Churchman, and supporter of what he calls 'religious education.' The whole strength of the clergy, publicans, bishops, loafers, avowed atheists, Roman Catholic archbishop, priests, and Irish is most heartily with the Church-loving, beer-brewing candidate, who is socially much liked, and very strong. His opponent is supported by the whole Liberal party, by large numbers of the Churchmen, and by a few Catholics. The Amended Education Act simply provides that whereas at present State aid is given to denominational schools it shall now be withdrawn. The Bible is not read in the schools, but the lesson books of the Irish National Schools are used. Facilities are offered to the various denominations to give religious instruction to the children in the State schools. The bishop and clergy of the Church of England and the Roman Catholic priests unite heartily with the beer interest (as usual), the proposal to tax the beer coming in very opportunely to enlist the sympathies and votes of the idle, drunken, venal, and dissolute portion of the community. The bishop takes an opportunity of stating publicly how much he is in favour of temperance, and his clergy follow suit; the Catholic clergy do the same, and in the evenings clergy of both religious denominations appear at public meetings in support of the brewer! The publicans and their followers are relieved from saying anything about the tax on beer by the existence of the education question, which they heartily oppose, thus avoiding the subject in which they have a selfish interest; so it comes to this—Bible says to beer, 'I'll support you, although it is rather inconvenient, for am I not pledged to temperance?' Beer says to Bible, 'I'll support you with all the strength of my lungs, rendered all the noisier by copious draughts of untaxed beer; beer and Bible, Bible and beer for ever!'

"The Roman Catholic clergy anathematise Protestants of all kinds and classes, including the Church of England, but the latter joins hands with the Roman Catholics and the beer party to gain its ends, the said ends being the same with both Churches—viz., the triumph of priestly rule and domination."

The answer of the constituency, applauded throughout the length and breadth of the land, was to return the Liberal candidate by a majority of two to one.

In reference to this election the *Sydney Morning Herald* said—" Many of the advocates for the extension and maintenance of the denominational schools lay great stress upon the doctrine that it is not 'just' to deny denominational schools to those who prefer them

—that if any citizen pays the education tax he ought to have the sort of education provided for his child that he most desires, and that it is a wrong-doing to his conscience if this claim is not regarded. It is certainly somewhat singular that the few advocates of this line of argument are to be found in the ranks of the two great churches, which, having been national churches, have, to say the least, not distinguished themselves by defending the rights of conscience. In England the march of religious liberty has done much to undo Church-inspired legislation against those outside the pale of the Church; and that being achieved it sounds strangely to hear the 'conscience' argument against a uniform treatment of all citizens proceed from a quarter which has not been the home of the rights of conscience."

A BULLOCK TEAM ON THE BLUE MOUNTAINS.

Before leaving Sydney it may be well to describe an overland ride I made from Sydney to Melbourne *via* Wagga Wagga and Albury, at a time previous to the completion of the through railway.

Leaving Sydney by the Pullman train at six in the evening, Wagga Wagga is reached about ten next morning. During the night we ascended 2,200ft. A large extent of the country is cleared, and, being New Year's Day, it was rather strange to our English eyes to see the wheat cut and stacked, and harvesting operations going on. The country through which our

Bush Hut.

track passes is famous for its sheep runs and for the high quality of the wool produced in it. Here and there in the bush are occasional labourers' cottages, wretched, uncomfortable looking buildings, constructed of rough planks covered with bark. The children we saw had a very uncared-for look.

Wagga Wagga (pronounced Wogga Wogga) covers a large extent of ground, but at present the number of houses is few, most of them, however, being well built. From this place we hired a buggy and pair of horses to take us to Albury, a distance of some seventy to eighty miles, the charge for which, including the services of a smart, bright boy as driver, was £7. Immediately on leaving Wagga we got into the "bush" country, and during the afternoon passed some large stock "stations." The land appears to be much more fertile than in the neighbourhood of Sydney, with greater depth of soil. We put up for the night at Jerra Jerra, a place consisting of two or three wood shanties, one of them being the hotel, and left at 6.30 next morning, taking breakfast at a somewhat larger group of wood huts called Germanton. Every driver through the "bush" makes his own track among the trees, and ours was no exception to the rule; he made long detours at intervals, only coming out into the regular road when a creek had to be crossed. We saw many pairs of large magpies, and some other birds which the driver informed us build large mud nests. Then the Great Ants, too, are very numerous, so that one dare not sit down anywhere to rest. The flies are also a great pest, and as my companion said, "won't take a hint," requiring to be toppled over before they will move. At about seven a.m. we passed the Royal Mail bowling along amongst the trees, our driver quickly making a fresh track to avoid the fearful dust which it raised. The coach is a big lumbering machine, painted flaring red, and drawn by six horses. It is licensed to carry sixty-five passengers, who can only be got on to it by being packed like herrings in a barrel. The weather being so hot and the dust so great, it must be terrible to be cooped up in it with fat people and thin, smokers and others. The coaches are hung upon enormous leather " springs," and they need them, for the road is so rough, and the coachmen are so daring, that the bumping and thumping are terrific. Each coach is fitted with four large reflector lamps, three in front and one behind.

While baiting the horses I had a chat with a farm labourer, who, like a great many of the immigrants with whom I have spoken, was sighing for old England again. He told me the ordinary farm labourer's wages here are 12s. to 15s. a week with board, and that 20s. a week is considered exceptionally good, while the great heat, dust, and reptiles are so troublesome that most of the labourers wish they were well out of it. This man told me his little terrier was killed by a snake a day or two before; the poor creature swelled up and died in great agony in ten minutes after being bitten; its death, however, was speedily avenged, his master killing the snake shortly afterwards. The landlady said she was in great terror of the snakes, which were very numerous. Near the run was a large log, and it was well known that a big black snake had taken up his abode there, for he was frequently seen to come out. In the winter season the reptile would very soon have been despatched by the same process adopted by the Chinaman when he wanted "roast pig," but this being summer, to fire the log meant to cause a general conflagration in the bush.

The power of endurance of Australian post-horses is something wonderful; yesterday we travelled more than thirty-five miles after one o'clock, over a rough bush road, or rather no road at all, bumping up and down in a way that must be very trying to the poor animals, as the "path" is never certain; and to-day we had to go nearly fifty miles more, the heat being intense, and the track covered with dust nearly a foot thick. Our driver, a mere lad of thirteen years, drove on with the greatest confidence, never having missed the

AN UP-COUNTRY TOWN.

way once, though there were no direction posts, and we did not come across a person or house once in ten miles, and were amongst the trees all the time. Towards evening the horses got rather tired, and so did poor "Tommy," the driver, who at times had a quiet "weep" to himself, but at last we reached Albury, and found our Melbourne friend awaiting us at the hotel.

For hours before, we had in view a fine range of hills, enclosing a large extent of country, including the valley along which the River Murray runs. Here we got the blue, purple, and roseate tints on the mountains to perfection, and as the sun was going down just as we entered the town I thought I had rarely seen a more delightful picture.

There is a thriving, well-to-do look about the place which is very enlivening, the houses being well built, with wide verandahs projecting from two storeys, the streets straight and wide, and planted on both sides with acacias, poplars, and several varieties of pines, the whole forming a veritable little paradise.

This being the great centre of the wine-growing industry we were desirous of visiting the vineyards and seeing the capacious cellars which are formed in the hills, and for which the district is somewhat celebrated, but our friend, being very anxious to get back to Melbourne, assured us there was "nothing to see here," and told us to wait till we got into Victoria, and so hurried us off.

We left Albury at 5.30 on the following morning, driving across the Murray to the railway station at Wodonga, the first town on the Victorian side, as Albury is the last on the New South Wales side, and the contrast between the two is great indeed—just the difference between prosperity and decay. New South Wales, with its Free Trade policy, is fitly represented by bright and shining Albury, while Victoria may well read a lesson from the decay and ruin into which Wodonga has fallen. I could not help thinking that a dozen such contrasts along the frontiers of the two States would do more than anything to settle the fate of Protection. Even the omnibus driver was full of the subject, pointing out to us as we rode along the difference between the two places.

The railway ride to Melbourne occupies eight hours, although the distance is only about 180 miles. On the way we passed through Euroa, the town which was "stuck up," *i.e.*, plundered, by the notorious Kelly and his gang. There were only four of these fellows in the gang, but such was the terror they inspired that they were able to rob a whole town in broad daylight, while a train was passing through the station close by the bank from which they took a considerable amount of cash. Having done this, they next ordered all the people into carts, and drove them some miles out of the town, ordering them not to stir for four hours under pain of death. Having secured their booty the scoundrels rode off, and for two years succeeded in eluding the vigilance of the police, although the Government offered a reward of £8,000 for their capture, alive or dead.

CHAPTER VI.

BEFORE leaving the subject of the Australian Colonies a few observations on the state of the labour market, and upon the social condition of the people, may be interesting.

In most of the Australian colonies Free Trade practically prevails, the exception being Victoria. In this colony the system of Protection is to be found in its most pronounced form, almost every imported article of manufacture being the subject of a heavy duty.

The avowed object of this system is to encourage immigration by offering a premium upon the manufacture of every article in considerable demand in the Colony. I do not know how far this object has been attained as concerns immigration, but it is an admitted fact, and one which is causing Victorian politicians much anxiety, that the colony fails to retain its population. One result about which there can be no question is that this fiscal policy is concentrating the population about the large towns, the city of Melbourne presenting the appearance of the chief town of an old and populous State. A ride in any direction into the country, however, soon discloses the real nakedness of the land as regards inhabitants, the fact being that a very small proportion of the immigrants ever get beyond the towns. An obvious consequence is that the natural resources of the country are greatly neglected, and the evil of this state of things will be apprehended when it is seen that the manufacturing population is increasing in a vastly greater ratio than the constituency upon which its trade depends. Under such conditions the dangers of the situation are seriously augmented when depression of trade occurs. Such a state of things arose before the building of the late Exhibition in Melbourne. The building trade and the mechanical industries in the city being in a stagnant state, large numbers of people found themselves out of employment, their attitude causing the Government some anxiety. The Exhibition was decided upon in the hope that its erection would provide employment until trade should revive. I asked one of the Commissioners of the Exhibition what would happen if trade did not revive on the completion of the building? He replied, "Oh, they shall take it down again, for it will be useless after the Exhibition is over." Surely a notable instance of the dog subsisting by eating its own tail.

A natural result of all this is to produce in the minds of the working classes a feeling that the Legislature ought to secure to them a constant supply of work at high rates of wages, altogether leaving out of consideration the inevitable effect of such a course in checking demand. Naturally, each class expects to receive the benefit of this policy, and it is not surprising that the example of the manufacturers in demanding Protection should be followed, and even bettered, by the working men.

A curious example of this occurred when I was in Australia. The streets of Melbourne, being very wide and long, are peculiarly well adapted for the introduction of tramways. A Bill was introduced into the House authorising the construction of an experimental line, but it had to be abandoned in consequence of the determined opposition of the cab drivers, the majority of whom own the vehicles which they drive. These men argued, naturally enough, that as manufacturing trades were protected against foreigners, their business also should be protected against competition in the only form in which it could arise. Doubtless this resistance will eventually be overcome, but not without leaving a sense of injustice.

While each class seeks to have the benefit of Protection for its own manufactures, it also seeks to obtain the benefits of Free Trade for the raw material and smaller accessories used in their production. At the time I am referring to, a Tariff Revision Commission was in session, and representatives of the various manufacturing trades were examined with the view of ascertaining whether any changes were desirable. In almost every case extensive additions to the duty were demanded, eliciting from some of the members of the Commission a reminder that on previous occasions the representatives of protected industries declared they only required the tax to be levied for a limited time in order to enable them to establish their business.

The Protectionist newspapers used every means to stir up the various trades to avail themselves of the opportunity the Commission afforded of making fresh claims.

It so happens that most of the materials used for newspaper printing are admitted duty free. The *Argus*, the leading journal in Victoria, and a consistent advocate of Free Trade, took this opportunity of suggesting that the proprietors of the Protectionist journals should prove the sincerity of their expressed opinions by appearing before the Commission and demanding the imposition of a tax upon newspaper materials in the interests of "native industry." Of course the suggestion was not adopted, perhaps for this reason, also suggested by the *Argus*, that the struggle for existence was already sufficiently severe.

The operative printers also demanded of the Commission that printed books should be more heavily taxed, one of their delegates remarking that "there was sufficient talent in Victoria to produce their own books," while a manufacturer, with great candour, asked for a little increase upon his special productions on the plea that his profit was not "quite enough!"

If profits are not enough prices are certainly sufficiently high, as the following instance will abundantly show. At the close of 1882 one hundred locomotives were required by the Government of Victoria, and although the needs of the country were most urgent—complaints of the inefficiency of the service coming in from all sides—the Protectionist party in the House demanded that the whole number should be made in the Colony, although there was only one firm who could undertake their manufacture, and that firm was unable to deliver the first engine under a period of ten months, and in addition to this, the total price demanded for the contract was £66,000 more than the engines could have been procured for without delay in England. It is admitted that the locomotives made in the Colony are much inferior to those imported, while in addition to the excess in first cost, the expense of maintaining the colonial engines is vastly greater. I was assured by competent authorities on the railways that the colonial engines are frequently under repair, and that their life is much shorter than that of their English rivals. The same evil principle is applied to the purchase of the miscellaneous stores supplied to the railways, thereby greatly enhancing the cost of working. Instances might be multiplied of the mischievous effects of a vicious fiscal policy in a young and undeveloped Colony. It is notorious that the great want of the Colonies is a larger population, and the Government in various ways—notably by making grants in aid of immigration—offer inducements to bring this result about. The manufacturers also require a larger field for their productions; but the working-class element is jealous of this very increase lest it should subject labour to competition, unmindful of the fact that there is ample room for an infinitely larger population.

Neither the agricultural nor the mining industries of the Colony are protected. As regards the former, public opinion would not permit the taxation of food; whilst, in the latter case, the minerals raised are, for the most part, exported, there being scarcely any demand for them in the Colony. But, while these industries receive no benefit from the fiscal policy of the Colony, they are heavily taxed in support of the revenue, for not only are all the machinery and materials used in their development subject to more than

25 per cent. import duty, but the cost of labour is greatly enhanced by the high wages, which become necessary when the purchasing power of money is diminished by Protection. Every year witnesses a considerable expansion of the industries in question ; and every year the cry becomes louder against the injustice and inequality of a system which places the natural resources of the country under so great a disadvantage. In consequence of the urgency of these complaints there is now some prospect of a reduction of the duty on agricultural and mining machinery.

I have met with men who were always ready to descant upon the advantages of Protection, but who, almost in the same breath, have told me they have never hesitated to evade the laws when they could do so to advantage, or even to break them when it suited their convenience and they could do so without much risk, justifying their conduct by saying that it was "quite right to cheat the Government when they could, because the Government were always ready to cheat them." In order to circumvent the practices of such men as these, the Legislature has been compelled to institute a complicated system of accounts in connection with the importation of goods, harassing in the last degree to those who have been accustomed to do business in a country where trade is unshackled.

In spite of the boasted advantages of Protection, it is evident that some manufacturers are not happy under it, as is shown by the fact of my having some time ago received from an important manufacturing firm in Victoria an application for my business agency in the Colony. In their application, the firm stated that the workpeople in the Colony were so very independent and so uncertain that they (the firm in question) would rather at any time sell imported articles at a smaller profit than manufacture them in their own works.

I have stated that the avowed objects of Protection were the attraction of a larger population and the fostering of "native industry." Now, with these very objects in view, the public men of New South Wales have from the first adopted and persisted in a policy diametrically opposed to that which has for years past been in force in the neighbouring Colony of Victoria. If the principles of Protection be sound, we should expect to find in the Free Trade Colony of New South Wales a state of things even much worse than I have shown to exist in Victoria. But what do we find? A constantly increasing population; abundance of employment; a vast and continually expanding railway system; shipping considerably greater than that of the Port of London one hundred years ago; an import and export trade greater than that of Great Britain at the same period; in short, every evidence of great and enduring prosperity.

As in America, "where acres are many and men are few," the manufacture of agricultural machinery has been brought to greater perfection than in almost any other country, so in Australia the same conditions have developed a flourishing manufacture of special machinery used in mining—one of the staple industries of the country. A demand for this improved machinery has recently sprung up in other countries, a considerable order having been received from India by an Australian firm while I was there.

In Sydney—not in spite of, but because of, Free Trade—the largest manufacturing concern in the Australian Colonies has grown up. The founders of this large business had the sagacity at the outset to recognise that there were certain articles which must of necessity be better and more cheaply made in the Colony than they could be imported. They put down steam saw-mills for supplying planking, which before had been imported; they next proceeded to make such articles as window-sashes, doors, frames, etc., for house-building, choosing such as could be manufactured almost entirely by machinery, which they obtained from England and America. By such natural means, and altogether free from legislative interference, they have built up the enormous business known as Hudson Brothers, Limited, railway rolling-stock manufacturers. It is clear that with the most improved machinery, purchased in the cheapest markets and imported duty free, and having inexhaustible supplies of native timber, not only cheaper but much better adapted to the climate than that hitherto imported, the opening for a perfectly legitimate business presented itself; in fact, they created a genuine "native industry." But Messrs. Hudson, recognising, as already pointed out, that other countries have also special advantages for the production of certain articles, wisely abstain from attempting a hopeless competition. For this reason they import such portions of the rolling-stock as wheels, axles, springs, carriage-furniture, etc.

The free importation of mining and agricultural machinery into New South Wales has given these industries such a stimulus that they have been more generally developed throughout that Colony than those of Victoria, causing a continuous and increasing demand for labour. The immigration into New South Wales is greatly in excess of that into Victoria; and, in addition to this, large numbers of artizans and others are continually crossing the border from the latter into the former Colony. In 1880, forty-five thousand persons arrived in New South Wales from other than Australian ports, and it is not too much to say that there is ample room for four times their number every year.

Until a few years since the great shipping companies had their repairing yards and shops in Victoria, but the extremely high cost of everything required by them compelled them at last to remove their establishments to her Free Trade neighbour, thereby effecting a very considerable saving. The same causes have doubtless been influential in securing to New South Wales the remarkable development of its shipping interests during the last generation.

So little is known in England of what our friends in the Colonies are doing, that probably many will be startled to learn that whereas in 1782 the total imports and exports of Great Britain amounted in value to about £23,350,000, in New South Wales, in 1881, the value was £27,650,000.

During the last thirty years the shipping annually arriving in Sydney has increased from

90 vessels, with a tonnage of 48,776, to
1,389 ,, ,, 973,425;

and the clearances in the same period increased from

47 vessels, with a tonnage of 24,081, to
1,322 ,, ,, 941,895.

During the last ten years, too, the population of New South Wales has increased 53 per cent., while that of Victoria has only increased 18 per cent., and while the excess of immigration over emigration in the former Colony has quadrupled, it has been almost stationary in the latter.

During the same period the Customs revenue in Victoria, notwithstanding the high tariff, has remained almost stationary; while in New South Wales, with a low tariff and smaller population, it has increased nearly one-half. The imports, too, have increased 80 per cent., against 17 per cent. in Victoria, and the exports 94 per cent. against 28 per cent.

These figures, taken from official papers in 1882, have never been dealt with by Victorian Protectionists, but are full of meaning to all those whom vested interests have not made blind. While it is true that Australia presents, and will continue to present, a great field for the surplus population of older countries, it is, in my opinion, a mistake to suppose that the upper grades of English artizans improve their position much by going there. Wages are higher it is true, and eight hours make up a day's work; animal food also is cheaper, but almost everything else is dearer than in England—house-rents, indeed, enormously so. An artizan who in Birmingham would be well housed for 5s. to 6s. a week would have to pay £1 for much inferior accommodation ; this remark applies generally in Australia, the principal cause being the great lack of artizans in the building trade. Many too, may consider the higher wages and shorter hours of labour as not too great a compensation for the exhaustion induced by the heat and dust of the climate and the annoyance from insect life. But for unskilled labour and for skilled agricultural labour there can be only one opinion, —viz., that the Colonies present a field where sobriety and industry are certain to bring a reward such as is altogether unattainable at home.

The education of the people is admirably provided for by the Legislature, every district being well supplied with first-rate schools, while the means of intercommunication by rail, post, and telegraph are superior to those of any country in the world, when the smallness of the population and the immense distances to be covered are taken into consideration.

In Australia, especially in the southern Colonies, there is happily no native question to absorb the attention of the people and to upset the calculations of financiers, consequently the colonists are able to devote all their energy to opening up the natural resources of the country. At the present time many millions of money are set aside for the construction of new railways and for the supply and storage of water, and when these are completed vast areas of agricultural land will be opened sufficient to accommodate all the spare population of England for many years to come.

If "Young Australia," like his cousin in America, has an unbounded confidence in the future of his country, he has even more in himself, as is well illustrated by the following story told me by an old resident. In one of the cities a number of young men had established a Debating Society, which met every Wednesday evening in a room in a narrow street. On the other side of the street was a church where service was held at the same time. The weather being hot the windows of both buildings were usually open, and the important deliberations of the young men were much interrupted by the preaching and singing in the church. With a delightful unconsciousness of what in slang phrase is called "cheek," they instructed their secretary to write to the minister of the church, requesting him to hold his service upon some other evening of the week!

The people of Australia are possessed of vast energy and great intelligence: and, having unlimited and well-grounded faith in their capacity to conquer the many difficulties which lie before them, are determined that their future career shall do no discredit to the great country from which they have sprung, and of whose history they are so proud.

The Duck-billed Platypus (*Ornithorhyncus paradoxus*).

SYDNEY HARBOUR.—GARDEN ISLAND.

CHAPTER VII.

E left Sydney in the first week in April, and although we had greatly enjoyed the beautiful scenery of its fine harbour and the neighbouring Blue Mountains, and had experienced the greatest kindness and hospitality on every side, we were not sorry to depart.

In the first place, we were homeward-bound, and I had recovered the health, in search of which I had left home and friends, and the weather had been so oppressively hot and the dust so troublesome, that we were glad of the prospect of the abatement of the one and the total disappearance of the other.

For ten months the Colony had had no rain, and in the neighbourhood of Sydney trees were dying by hundreds, and gardens which had been carefully tended for fifteen or twenty years were nearly spoiled. The outlook for agriculturists was dark indeed, very indifferent hay was selling for £10 a ton, and the cattle were perishing for want of water. I saw a statement in the paper that one farmer had already lost 45,000 sheep, and if the drought lasted a few weeks longer he would lose 50,000 more. The most inveterate grumbler at the moisture of the English climate would, if here in Sydney, soon arrive at the conclusion that six months' rain is to be preferred to ten months' drought and dust under a scorching sun.

Some friends accompanied us on board our steamer, and observing that the sky had become overcast with every prospect of a heavy downpour, I endeavoured to persuade them to return to shore, but they said the sky often looked overcast but soon became clear again, and that there would be no rain; still I was not comfortable, and presently induced them to go. Half-an-hour afterwards our time was up, the ship's gun was fired, and down came the rain in such torrents as made me very apprehensive for the safety of my friends, lest their boat should be swamped. On arriving at New York I found a letter from them informing me that the rain filled the boat so fast that it was with some difficulty they could keep it afloat.

Our vessel was an exceedingly fine one, and was on her first voyage. Her length was 400ft. and she was 40ft. wide across the saloon. The appointments seemed to be all very good, although it soon appeared that she was insufficiently supplied with stewards, the consequence being that the meals were badly served. Everything, however, was done according to rule, and it was curious to see the order in which the various dishes were brought in. The chief steward rang a bell once, and the stewards marched into the saloon in single file, dishes in hand; two rings, right wheel;

three times, place dishes on the table; and at the fourth ringing of the bell, remove covers and march out with them. It looked like a pantomime, and caused us considerable merriment. The head steward was a negro, and it was curious to note how he lorded it over the white stewards.

A rough passage of four days brought us to the entrance of Auckland harbour. The previous day it was very stormy, and an albatross which had been following us for some time, frequently flying across the ship between the masts, at length either flew, or was blown, against one of the masts, and fell dead upon the deck.

In approaching the town of Auckland a number of islands of curious shape, surmounted with rocks bearing the appearance of castles, are passed. Auckland looks well from the harbour, which is a very fine one; behind the town a mountain rises to a considerable altitude, greatly adding to the picturesqueness of the view.

Our ship was the largest that had ever been in the harbour, and we expected soon to have a number of boats plying for hire, but none appeared until half our limited time had expired, and consequently very few passengers went ashore. We took a quantity of coal on board, the quality of which was very bad, giving off volumes of the densest smoke. It is much inferior to the New South Wales coal, which in its turn is not equal to English.

For the first ten days the Pacific greatly belied its name, being in a state of great commotion the whole time; indeed, most of the way to San Francisco the roll was very considerable. As we neared Kandavu, in the Fiji Islands, the dreaded coral reefs began to come in sight. Some of them stretch out for fifteen miles from the land, and are known to approaching vessels by the white crests of the long lines of breakers. Navigation is very dangerous, and the harbour of Kandavu is a very difficult one to make. Just before entering we passed within fifty feet of the masts of a sunken ship; but, having brought a native pilot from Sydney, we got inside safely. The harbour is exceedingly beautiful. For some distance from the water on each side the ground is covered with cocoa-nut and bread-fruit trees, large ferns, and a great variety of bright green foliage, while beyond is a range of hills of beautiful shapes and well wooded.

It being Sunday only two or three boats made their appearance, the missionaries not permitting the natives to come out to trade or to gratify their curiosity on that day. Knowing this we were not a little amazed to receive a visit presently from the missionaries themselves, who were rowed by eight very intelligent natives, having no clothing worthy of mention. Some of our party taxed the missionaries with their lack of consistency, and were answered that they came " by invitation." The natives have fine open faces, with good foreheads, bright and restless eyes. They are of a dark chocolate or liver colour. Their hair is very abundant, but they spoil it by putting quicklime upon it, turning it to a dirty reddish brown. Their vivacity is astonishing. They laugh and chatter in a ceaseless chorus, but their language is not musical. One old fellow was particularly voluble; he was in a boat, and was giving instructions to his crew in a fearfully loud voice, which sounded like the slipping of a ship's cable through the hawser-hole.

A NATIVE OF FIJI.

It was great fun to watch the children diving for money. If you threw a sixpence into the water they would go after it and catch it before it had gone down many feet, quickly reappearing to ask—like Oliver Twist—for more, and with a grin, disclosing teeth which made us envy them.

Some of our fellow-passengers went ashore, and were much charmed with all they saw. The little children very much delighted them by coming up and putting their hands into those of their visitors, leading them off to show them the bread-fruit and banana trees.

Just as daylight was going our gun was fired, and with our pilot on board we steamed out of the harbour, having the pilot's boat in tow, manned with as merry a crew as ever rowed a boat. The captain was very anxious to get clear of the reefs before dusk, and so went at a pretty good speed, and although the pilot-boat was half out of the water, and was constantly being swamped, the crew laughed and shrieked with delight, shouting and making curious noises like Christy Minstrels.

Presently they commenced a song, one old fellow beating time with an oar—but we preferred the shrieking. Soon the pilot clambered down the ship's side, and after giving him three cheers we set off at full speed.

There are many sharks in these waters, but it is said they are not fond of the dark skins. Whether that is so or not I do not know, but certainly both boys and men disregard the presence of these monsters in diving for money.

The day after leaving Kandavu we passed through a beautiful group of islands surrounded with coral reefs. We passed so close to two of these islands that we were able to see the cocoa-nut trees quite distinctly, the bright green vegetation rising just above the pure white surf, and the whole surrounded by the glorious purple and azure of the ocean. While passing one of the islands we saw a huge waterspout burst, and were glad our ship was well out of it.

Soon after leaving the Fiji Islands the crew were put through fire-brigade practice. The bell was rung continuously, the whistles blown, and the crew and stewards rushed to the fire-engines, and got out the buckets and hose, and soon began playing over the ship, while the first officer superintended the getting out and lowering of the boats. As very few persons were warned of what was going to be done, there was naturally great excitement amongst the passengers, one lady fainting in the saloon, thinking the ship was really on fire. I was not impressed with the smartness or efficiency of either officers or crew, and was devoutly thankful that there was no need for their services; and yet I often wondered there were no fires, there being so many kerosene lamps all over the ship, to say nothing of the immense kitchen fires, where twice in one morning I saw a regular burst of flame through an unskilful cook overturning the fat in the absence of his chief.

In going from England to Australia, and returning *via* the Pacific, and across America, one day is gained, and in order to keep our calendar right we had to "drop a day," or when we arrived at Liverpool we should be a day in advance of our home friends. This is done by having two days of the same name and date in one week. It appears rather curious but is plain enough, for our general course since leaving home was eastward, and continued so until we reached home. Now, as in going east, four minutes to each degree are gained (the reverse in going west), it follows that in the 360 degrees into which the earth's circumference is divided, a total gain of $360 \times 4 = 1,440$ minutes, or 24 hours is made.

Our doctor was somewhat of a curiosity. One evening he told me that one of the passengers, who was suffering from an ailment of the eyes, had declined his further services, preferring to pay one of the passengers who was a medical man. He assured me he had no feeling about it, he was quite above that sort of thing. "Our profession," he said, "is one in which we should always practice the virtue of charity in accordance with the teaching of Christ, whose follower I trust I am." But observing that during the conversation he frequently swore, I gave him a hint about it. "Ah," said he, "you remind me of my little wife at home; whenever I swear or consign any one to a warm place, she puts her finger up and says, 'Ah, don't do that, you know you don't mean it,' which of course is perfectly true, so there is no harm in it." One of our doctors was re-named a "compound-conceited-cuss-of-a-colonial-cockatoo-quack-of-a-doctor." He believed in the Australian "spread eagle"—in the cockatoo, that is—and had visions of a time when England would be a "foreign" country. But he was labouring under the impression that there were eight millions of people in the Australian colonies, whereas there were not more than $2\frac{1}{2}$ millions of white, black, yellow, and brown.

Life on shipboard is not more free from little personal difficulties than on land: one of our colonial friends daily raised the susceptibilities of his neighbours at the dinner table by emptying a favourite dish of fruit into his pocket for home consumption; while just before reaching Honolulu it was rumoured there was to be a duel as soon as we arrived at the island. One of the English travellers had an objectionable habit of turning the fruit over with his fingers at dessert, and picking out the best. A colonial gentleman frequently rebuked him mildly for his breach of good manners, telling him he should "touch and take"; and so it resulted in a quarrel which it was said "blood alone can quell." It is satisfactory, however, to know that the deadly encounter did not come off.

Being told by the Captain that we might expect to land at Honolulu at 6 p.m., the four o'clock dinner table was comparatively deserted, most of the passengers preferring to reserve themselves for what the Yankees call a "good square meal" on shore. We arrived off the entrance to the harbour in good time, and made the usual signals for a pilot, but with no result. After sunset, guns and rockets were fired, but no pilot appearing, the Captain decided to run in without one. In consequence of the delay it was ten o'clock before we landed, when we found the islanders were *en fête*, and were informed that on such occasions the pilots decline to go out for vessels. Just as we were about to land, one of our passengers, in the darkness, fell overboard, but being a good swimmer and a strong, fearless man, he managed to get aboard again, with no worse result than a wetting. This gentleman had the reputation of being somewhat of a sceptic, and that afternoon I had been discussing with him the subject of a future state. When he was safe on deck again I reminded him of our conversation, and asked what his thoughts were when under the water in such a perilous situation. He replied, "I will tell you exactly what I did think. When I fell overboard I had three shillings in my hand, and my first thought when under water was as to their safety; so, before doing anything else, I safely deposited them in my pocket, and then proceeded to 'go aloft.'" On landing we found ourselves amongst a motley throng, whose faces, however, were too dark to be seen, the majority dressed in light coloured raiment, and all laughing, shouting, jabbering and shrieking in a ten times more lively manner than a mob of gay Neapolitans on the arrival of a train at Naples. We found the hotel about a mile from the landing place, and very much enjoyed the walk along the wide unpaved streets, lined with houses of various shapes and sizes, many with gardens around them. Myriads of fire-flies lit up the darkness, and the air was laden with the perfume of tropical flowers. On arriving at the hotel, we found it to be a spacious, well-lighted building, with lofty reception rooms, through which we wandered in quest of waiters to whom to give our orders for supper, but no servant could we find, neither could we get any response to the bells, which were vigorously rung by a hungry crowd. We made our way to the office, and were there informed that we could get nothing to eat till next morning, as the servants had "gone home," and nothing was served after nine o'clock. It was in vain we declared we were starving; the only reply was that we could get what we liked to *drink* at the bar. A Yankee standing by, pitying our plight, said it was quite true we could get nothing that night, but told us how we could be the first to be served in the morning. He recommended us to order our breakfast at the office before leaving, and to pay for it there and then, and to be at the hotel again before seven o'clock next morning. This we did, and then returned to the vessel, where we also were too late to obtain anything to eat. In the morning we were early at the hotel (buying some delicious strawberries on the way), and proceeding to the breakfast room, were informed we could not obtain admission until seven o'clock. At the appointed hour the folding doors were opened by two natives of the "Flowery Land," and we were soon seated at the tables, which were crowded with a bountiful supply of most tempting viands, and quantities of luscious fruit.

As soon as all the seats were occupied the Celestial waiter closed the door, and was most assiduous in seeing that his staff attended carefully to the wants of his guests. Presently there were loud knockings at the door, to which no attention whatever was vouchsafed by the smiling Chinee; and when the knockings were varied by angry exclamations from our friends outside, his face became blander still. It could not be said of this "Heathen Chinee" that his "tricks they were vain," for they were only too effectual in keeping the hungry crowd at bay. When we had quite finished (and I fear we were in no haste to depart), the doors were opened to admit a further batch of impatient voyagers, and even then only one half of the expectant throng could be admitted, the remainder being advised to betake themselves to the restaurants in the town. We shall not soon forget our experiences at the Honolulu Hotel, the landlord of which is no less a personage than His Most Gracious Majesty the King of the Hawaiian Islands.

We occupied the remainder of the limited time at our disposal in walking and driving around the town and neighbourhood.

The date and other palms, india-rubber and cocoa-nut trees, tree ferns, guavas, and other kinds of tropical vegetation flourish here in great abundance. Flowers of the most brilliant colours grow everywhere, and the houses of the better classes seem perfect little paradises, with numerous jets of water flying. The grass is delightfully green and beautiful, and great dragon-flies flit about in all directions. Here and there we came across a group of little black-eyed, brown-faced, merry children, looking shyly at the white strangers, and rushing wildly along the streets. We also met numbers of natives on horseback, dressed in splendid colours—red, blue, yellow, and green—all mixed, or in masses of one or more of these delicate hues. "Will you ride," said one. "Not to-day" I said, "perhaps to-morrow." "That no good," replied he, "for steamer sails to-morrow!" and off he went at a gallop. They are sharp, sprightly fellows, very handsome, wonderfully lithe and active, and have dark, flashing eyes.

The women of the labouring class are very stately looking, and walk with a dignity and grace a duchess might envy. Their clothing is not of a very extensive character, consisting apparently of one long loose robe, gathered neatly around the neck and wrists, with gay-coloured ribbons, and suggesting the idea that seven years would be an unnecessary time for a Honolulu girl to be bound to learn dressmaking.

Meeting a number of little girls returning from school, I tried to get them to come and read to us out of their books. They were very shy, and it was some time before they would venture near us. At last one of them let me have her book, and I saw that her name was Emma—after the good queen of that name, who visited England a few years since—so I said, "Now, Emma, read us something, and I will give you this," holding a new threepenny piece before her. At once she came and read a page in the true conventional schoolgirl monotone. The book was printed in Honolulu, and was in the native language, which sounded sweet, and free from harshness. She was a nice-looking little girl, quite a "brownie," and was much pleased with her threepenny-piece. The children were delighted at seeing Queen Victoria's face on the coin, and frequently repeated her name. The race is fast dying out, and in a few generations will become extinct.

During the day we visited a school, and looked over the Parliament House, which is a handsome building. The hall is very large and lofty, and so also are the rooms, the walls and ceilings being lined with a smooth white enamel. In connection with the House of Parliament there is a tolerably good library, and the nucleus of a good museum, but the country is very poor; indeed I am told it is almost bankrupt. On passing the post-office it occurred to us to ask if there were any letters for us, although we did not expect any, and putting our cards on the table we said we supposed there were no letters for us. "Oh, but there are though," the clerk said, "and I am very glad to get rid of them," whereupon, to our intense delight, he produced a huge packet of letters and papers.

While driving into the country we passed many pretty villas, with gardens full of splendid shrubs and flowers, and on to a native village. The houses are made chiefly of large rushes, which grow here in great

RUTH, THE KING'S SISTER (Died 1883).

abundance. There seem to be no chairs or seats in the houses, every one squatting on the ground. We passed some native women carrying their babies, and I asked if they would sell me one. "Yes, for a dollar," one replied; but when I said " Very well, then, bring it here," she altered her mind, which was a good thing for me, for I should not have known what to do with a black baby.

The temperature of Honolulu ranges between 60° and 88°, and the islands are always fanned by the N.E. trade winds, rendering them exceedingly healthy.

Our visit conveyed the impression to our minds that it would be impossible to spend a month more delightfully than among the Hawaiian group, and we bade adieu to Honolulu with the greatest regret.

It was a beautiful moonlight evening when we left Honolulu for San Francisco, and after many months' travelling by land and sea, we began to feel that we were at last really homeward bound, for would not our *next* voyage land us at Liverpool? While at Honolulu we received a very considerable addition to our passenger list in the persons of a number of Americans, of both sexes, some of them being gentlefolks and some of them not. We also took on board three thousand bundles of bananas, which were hung up in the netting all round the promenade deck. This was a most unfair arrangement on the part of the captain, as not only were the seats on this deck rendered unavailable, and a large portion of the space occupied, but the ship became overrun with centipedes, some of them five inches long, making it like Egypt during one of the plagues, " for they were in all our quarters," in our beds and in our clothes. Americans, as a rule, are not good sailors. Hence it is that when commencing a voyage they take it for granted that they are going to be ill, and make their arrangements accordingly. My companions had been flattering themselves that the spare berth in their cabin would remain empty to the end of the voyage, but they were doomed to disappointment, for it was their bad fortune to receive one of the most bilious-looking of the new arrivals. On entering the cabin the first observation the Yankee made was, "Where d'ye throw up?" The answer to which was, "We don't 'throw up' at all. We *go* up and lean over the lee side." The event proved the Yankee's apprehensions to be well founded. One party of Americans were returning from a prolonged residence on one of the islands of the Pacific, where they appeared to have acquired some of the native habits. One day these people were taking their lunch on deck; it consisted of chicken and a native dish called "poi." The latter was a substance like bill-stickers' paste, and was contained in a large bowl. The company, which numbered some five or six persons, men and women, sat upon the deck around the bowl, and, having learned from their new acquaintances, the savages, to do without spoons and separate dishes, helped themselves to the delicious mixture by each dipping two fingers into the common bowl until it was empty. They then attacked the chicken, and had evidently taken lessons in carving from the same authorities, for they adopted the primitive plan of pulling it to pieces. Of course these proceedings excited considerable remark among the passengers, but the party seemed quite insensible to observation.

Another of our passengers was an American, named Steinberg, who had a grievance against the British Government on account of an alleged outrage on the part of an English man-of-war's crew, in some dispute in the Samoan Islands. He was nursing his wrath until he arrived at Washington, when he certainly thought England's fate would be settled, and that she would be "chawed up catawampously." This man was accompanied by a Yankee journalist of a most anti-British type. He was a sallow-faced man with a large, square lower jaw, without any hair on his face, and with straight lanky locks, and, moreover, was something under five feet high. He was so thorough-going in his hatred of everything British that when " God save the Queen " was sung at the close of a concert in the saloon, he got up with much fuss and stalked out, followed by some half-dozen of his countrymen. We called the fiery editor "Jefferson Brick," after Martin Chuzzlewit's acquaintance. On one occasion I heard a friend of this gentleman ask him if he had a chair on deck. He said he had not, as the Britishers always brought a good supply. I took the hint, and determined that, at any rate, he should not use mine. Soon afterwards it happened that a sea, breaking over the deck, soaked the carpet seat of my chair, which obliged me to place it in a sunny position that it might dry. Presently I saw " Mr. Brick " deliberately fetch the chair, which was a very comfortable one, and, taking it into the shade, settle down on it. I went to him and remarked that the chair was quite wet. "I guess it's dry now," said he, with the peculiar twang of a down-east Yankee. Seeing that he failed to take the hint, I told him that the chair was mine and that I would thank him to give it up. This he did, with a remark that he "did not see what people who were always walking about wanted with chairs at all."

We were not altogether without curious examples of our own countrymen as fellow-passengers. One in particular, an Irish tradesman, from one of the New Zealand ports, seemed determined to amuse and be amused. We called our friend "Mister," because he addressed everybody by that name. It appears that "Mister" was too fond of liquor, and that he had to take an occasional holiday, in order to give his friends an opportunity of putting his affairs straight at home. I was told that he had a flourishing business, which was managed by two able assistants, who insisted upon his leaving them for twelve months in the interest of the concern, under the penalty, if he returned, of their opening an opposition shop. "Mister" told me he had been educated in four Colleges in Ireland, which, doubtless, accounted for the remarkable absence of knowledge he displayed. He frequently alarmed us by the disappearance of the knife down his throat at the dinner table. One evening he volunteered to read at one of the entertainments in the saloon, and caused great amusement by the richness of his humour and of his brogue—winding up his reading by the impromptu observation, "and shure it is oi that am moighty droy." We shall hear of "Mister" again when we get to San Francisco.

One of our passengers, who died during the voyage, had been suffering greatly from severe pains in the head. He had been told by a lady that sometimes great relief was obtained in such cases by rubbing brandy upon the head. Soon after giving this advice the lady was walking down the saloon where there were a number of passengers and stewards, when she was astonished by hearing the poor invalid calling after her in the most excited manner, and to the no small wonderment of the passengers, "Miss, Miss, did you say brandy or whiskey?" On one occasion the doctor was examining this patient, when the poor fellow appealed to him to do what he could for him, saying, "Doctor, I should like to have one more chance, do you see, and if you can put this old crazy machine together again and make it run once more I shall take it—*as a personal favour!*" Before he became dangerously ill the invalid was in the same cabin with one of my friends, who one night was considerably disturbed by his dreadful coughing, varied at intervals by strong language respecting the cough, which, he declared, did not belong to him. "It's not mine, I never had a cough, it's my head that's wrong—this cough belongs to some other fellow; what's it bothering me for?" and when some ladies gently remonstrated with him he said, "Look here, now, I guess it's just as natural for me to swear as it is for you to pray!" His end came suddenly at last, and in a few hours after, in the early morning, his remains were

"In the deep bosom of the ocean buried."

We sighted the entrance to the magnificent harbour of San Francisco at daybreak on a beautiful morning at the end of April, and when we approached it the sun had just risen, bathing the whole scene in a flood of golden light, fully justifying its name, "The Golden Gate." In a short time the city came in view, reminding me very forcibly of Sheffield, from the dense masses of smoke which hung over a large portion of it, for San Francisco is an important manufacturing place. Soon we were boarded by a motley crew, composed of

Custom House officers, hotel-touts, porters, agents for the railway, and a number of keen-eyed gentry, desirous of earning a cent anyway, honest or otherwise. We had decided upon going to the famous Palace Hotel, and having found the agent, placed our luggage under his care, receiving checks for it, and, locking our cabin, proceeded on shore, where we found the most sumptuous omnibus we had ever seen waiting to convey passengers to the hotel.

THE HOTEL.—HONOLULU.

AMERICA.

CHAPTER VIII.

HE Palace Hotel in San Francisco is quite a town in itself, containing as it does over a thousand rooms, and with rarely less than a thousand inhabitants, including servants, only a limited number of the latter, however, living in the house. The establishment has its own gas-works, four artesian wells, affording an abundant supply of the purest water; it also possesses a thoroughly good fire-brigade, and an efficient system of police. There are five hydraulic lifts for the conveyance of guests and luggage to each floor of the house. The rooms on the ground floor are 25ft. high, and of corresponding size, the breakfast room being 110ft. by 58ft., the dining room 150ft. by 55ft., the walls being hung with excellent copies of the best works of the great masters. The corridors are lined and paved with white marble, and the grand staircase is of the same material.

The bedrooms are very large and airy, and they all have comfortable dressing-rooms attached, with hot and cold water supply, and with a dozen beautiful towels—a very refreshing sight to the voyager who has been cooped up for the previous month in the limited space allotted to passengers on an ocean steamer. The bedrooms have baths adjoining them, each bath being arranged for two rooms; there is also a service-room on each landing, where a dusky negro is always in attendance. Upon each landing there is a tube for the conveyance of letters for the post direct into the letter-box at the general office. There is also a pneumatic despatch-tube for the conveyance of messages and parcels to and from any point on the different floors. Upon the garden floor of the hotel there is an arcade promenade 12ft. wide, with entrances to all the shops under the hotel, upon the street level, each shop having a show window upon this promenade. There are three inner courts, the centre one being 140ft. by 84ft., covered with glass of the same height as the roof of the hotel. It has a carriage and promenade entrance from the street of 44ft. in width, and a circular carriage way of 54ft. in diameter, which is surrounded by a marble-tiled promenade and a tropical garden. The garden is well supplied with exotic plants, statuary, and fountains. Around this centre court and upon every storey there is an open gallery from which all the bedrooms are entered, and from which they receive light and fresh air. The dining rooms are fitted with a large number of small tables for parties of from four to eight persons, an arrangement very much superior to the long tables in most *salles à manger*.

There are about four hundred waiters, one-fourth only being white men, the rest negroes. The latter seem specially adapted for waiting, being active and nimble, and seeming to anticipate every wish. They receive £1 per week wages and their board, but lodge away from the house. A fresh bill of fare is printed daily for each meal, and the variety of food is very great, there being a choice of about seventy dishes at dinner. In the kitchen are twenty-seven French cooks, besides assistants—a sufficient guarantee for the excellent manner in which the food is prepared.

There is a splendid laundry in the house, where the washing is done by fifty Chinese washer*men*, and certainly never was linen more exquisitely got up than here. These Celestials are specially successful in all kinds of starching requiring a smooth polished surface, such as shirt fronts. The mode in which they apply the starch is quite novel, for having taken a mouthful they blow it out on to the article in a continuous fine spray, while their hands are occupied in ironing.

The servants take their meals in *table d'hote* fashion, being waited on by a batch of their fellow servants, and everything is conducted with the greatest possible regularity and order. I was much pleased to find that all the gas and water fittings, also the hydraulic lifts and pumps, were supplied by English makers, and were such as to command the admiration of everybody.

An American gentleman, hearing me speak of the hotel, asked me how I liked it? I told him I was greatly delighted with it; that it was a palace, indeed, in all its arrangements, but that in one respect I had been not a little astonished at what I had seen there—the presence of the extreme of civilisation face to face with a very close approach to barbarism. "How is that," said he. "Why," I replied, "you are only supplied with one knife and fork at meals; each guest has to dip his fishy knife into the butter, and the same process has to be gone through in taking salt and mustard; and seeing it is the fashion amongst the American guests to put the knife into their mouths, the idea is not pleasant."

I referred, too, to another peculiarity of the Americans arising, I believe, from their extensive use of the Virginian weed in chewing, and I said that the guests at the Palace Hotel, in passing through its marble halls, had not the same excuse for their conduct that the old Greek philosopher had when he was being shown over the palace by Crœsus, and when he excused himself for an unparalleled act of rudeness by saying "that such was the magnificence on every hand that the face of the king was the meanest thing that presented itself," for the proprietor of the hotel had made the most ample provision for the national habit—a provision which was, however, very generally disregarded.

The city of San Francisco is exceedingly well situated, and possesses many handsome streets, extensive hotels, and public buildings, but in none of these respects, save only in hotels, is it equal to Melbourne, though the evidences of great business activity and prosperity are much greater in the former city.

The day after I arrived at the hotel I was surprised at receiving the following letter:—"Dear Tangye,— Should you wish to see me I am to be found at the above address, or a letter addressed to me, Box 339, Post Office, will reach me promptly. My wife is dead. A. J. C. Jarratt." The name was quite strange to me, so I decided *not* to go, but to send a friend. My friend found the address, which was a wretched room at the top of a lofty pile of buildings, and after a few minutes' conversation with the man he saw there, was very glad to get into the street again, not liking the aspect of things. The following day, whilst seated at dinner with my friends, a waiter came to us and asked which was Dr. L——. On being told, he said a messenger from the chief of police was in waiting, wishing to see him. I looked at the doctor and asked him what he had been doing. Having finished our dinner we adjourned to the office and found the officer, who said his chief had received a telegram from a man in some town a hundred miles inland requesting him to send "his friend the Doctor" up to him as soon as possible. Of course my friend, knowing nothing whatever of the man, declined to go up country. I mentioned these polite attentions to a gentleman who was dining at the same table, and who I found was the leading lawyer in the city. He told me it was a favourite dodge with the sharpers, and that they sometimes caught a "flat" in this way. On the arrival of ocean steamers it is the custom to publish the names of the passengers in the evening papers, which accounts for the familiarity of these fellows with the names of strangers. We had many amusing chats with this lawyer. He remarked one day that I must have met with a deal of "character" in travelling. "Yes," I said, "I had, both good and bad." "Wa-a-l, I guess its better to meet with a *bad* character than none at all." Speaking of the neighbouring State of Nevada, which was still in a very unsettled condition, he said a friend of his was Governor there, and that he "was 6ft. 6in. in height, and had a number three head and a number fifteen foot, for" said he, "I guess weight of foot is more important there than weight of brain."

There are sharp men of business in the city who do not require offices in which to carry on their business. If you are walking in the streets with a friend, and, meeting someone else, stop for a chat, you will see a 'cute-looking fellow stop, and though he appears to be intent on something on the opposite side of the street, you will note that he is leaning his ear towards you, doubtless with the laudable intention of gaining a little information. On one occasion we met one of these individuals. He kept his ear open, and then struck in with "I guess you are going through to England. I can put you up to the best way of doing it and calculate I can save you from forty to fifty dollars on the job." We say we are much obliged, and will perhaps "call again." Then as you proceed along the streets attenuated fellows, with scanty, pointed beards and Mother Shipton hats, accost you with "Going east, gentlemen? Guess you'll want to change some money. Come with me, gentlemen, and I'll take you to the right place." "Thank you," we say, "not to-day." "Wa-a-l, guess exchange will go against you to-morrow, gentlemen." Observing on the door of a very handsome house a brass name-plate with the name "Mrs. Doctor Sanders," our guide informed us that there were many lady doctors in the city, and that they had very extensive practice.

The Chinese are very numerous in San Francisco, there being more than 40,000 of them there. At the time of my visit, the feeling of the rowdies ran very high against the Celestials, and threats of wholesale massacre were freely used against them. John Chinaman is a most industrious, frugal man, spending very little upon his living, and nothing upon his pleasures, always excepting his infatuation for opium. His needs being few, he can afford to work for very small pay, and thus comes into competition with the white workman. This is the head and front of his offending, but it is aggravated by the fact of his being equally skilful as an artificer. While the artizans have their special grievances about the Chinese, the wealthy classes have theirs also. It is true "John" does his master's work well and cheaply, but, as I have said before, he is not a spending man; his sole object is to get what the Yankees call "his little pile" as quickly as possible, and then return to his native land. Nor is this surprising when we consider that every Chinaman leaves his little "Min-ne" behind him when he quits the Flowery Land, it being a very rare thing for a woman to leave China.

The Chinese quarter is full of interest; the people swarm like bees, and live in a frightfully overcrowded state. The butchers' and barbers' shops are the most numerous and most interesting, the former being filled with a quantity of dreadful-looking little portions of meat, but it would puzzle the most learned to say from what animal they were cut. The barbers' shops are situated in the basements of the houses, with an open front towards the street, and they are very numerous, for the Chinese are close shavers. On looking down you may see a number of men seated in a variety of positions, each one smoking a pipe of opium, while the barber is occupied in shaving every portion of his head and face, excepting, of course, his beloved pig-tail. The swell Chinee is very particular that every hair shall be removed, and so clever do the operators become that, by means of tiny razors, they can shave the inside of the nose. Some of the pig-tails are of enormous length, and sometimes the white rowdies attack the Chinese and cut their pig-tails off.

The Chinaman (from a sketch by the Author).

When a man has an especially fine one, he either rolls it up at the back of his head and fastens it with hair-pins, or else tucks it inside his blouse. I noticed one of the latter in particular, a glimpse of which would have delighted Darwin himself. The owner had evidently let down his back hair before putting on his blouse, and consequently the pig-tail, which disappeared at the back of the neck, emerged from under the blouse and extended to his heels.

Some of our party, wishing to explore the Chinese quarter by night, engaged a detective to accompany them, it being unsafe to go unless so escorted. The guide first took them over a lodging house, in which some hundred Chinamen were stowed away, literally almost as thick as herrings in a barrel. Not only was the floor thickly covered, but suspended above it was a layer in hammocks, some smoking opium and others sleeping, none, however, taking the slightest notice of the intruding party.

LITTLE MIN-NE.

On visiting the Chinese theatre during the evening they found preparations being made to celebrate a Celestial wedding. This decided them to stay and see the ceremony, which was attended by a vast number of Chinese, the theatre being crowded in every part. After the ceremony most of the spectators formed in the procession, which escorted the happy pair to their home. My friends also visited the Joss Houses and inspected the queer-looking gods contained in them.

While making some purchases in a Chinese shop it was necessary to give my address. I wrote it out on a card thus—TANG-YE, upon which the Celestial at once claimed me as a countryman of his. I disabused his mind of that idea by putting my fingers to the outer corners of my eyes and pretending to extend them in an upward direction, the absence of which peculiarity showed conclusively that I was not of the true Mongol type. Curiously, however, on afterwards consulting a gazetteer, I found that there is in China a city named TANG-Y, containing over 30,000 inhabitants.

The Chinese are accused of having brought with them a number of objectionable practices, but to anyone possessing a knowledge of the lower classes in American cities, it will not appear possible that the Chinese can be very much worse than they.

Most of the traffic in San Francisco is carried on by the tramways, and it may not be out of place to put intending visitors on their guard with respect to a little peculiarity in their management. It is advisable to tender the exact fare if possible, for if you give a larger sum the balance is returned to you, not in cash, but in tickets available for future rides, which you may have no opportunity of taking. The hackney carriages are very fine, being almost equal to English private carriages. Most of those I saw were splendidly horsed with a pair of magnificent animals, generally black. The lowest fare taken is ten shillings, but I am bound to say you can have full value for your money in the time and the accommodation given you.

On Sunday morning the city presents a very lively aspect. The fire-brigades and volunteers parade the streets, preceded by their bands, and thousands of people go by tramway and other vehicles to see the famous sea-lions at the entrance to the bay. From the grounds in front of Cliff House they are seen on the rocks below in large numbers, tumbling about and making a noise like the barking of dogs, but so loud as to be heard from a distance of nearly a mile.

The climate is a delightful one, the temperature being singularly equable, ranging, as it does, in summer from 60° to 70°, and in winter from 50° to 60° Fahr. Indeed the weather is so beautiful that one cannot help referring to it frequently, but the invariable reply to any such observation is, "Well, I guess we shall have three months just the same right slick away."

SEAL ROCKS, SAN FRANCISCO.

After nearly a fortnight's stay at the Palace Hotel, enjoying its good fare, we began to think it time to move eastward, as we were getting too luxurious in our habits. My friend the lawyer, however, remarked that we need have no fear on that account, as the fare on the Pacific Railway would cure the severest attack of gout. Before leaving San Francisco we met our old friend "Mister" twice. From a report in the newspapers we learnt that he had been brought before the magistrates and fined for carrying fire-arms in the streets. "Mister" told us the police had taken all his money on the pretence of taking care of it for him. When we last saw him he was leaning against a lamp-post, helplessly drunk.

The Last of "Mister" (from a sketch by the Author).

The great excursion from San Francisco is of course to the Yosemite Valley, but we were compelled to forego the pleasure of making it on account of our visit being too early in the season. Some of our fellow-voyagers from the Colonies ventured to go, but, unfortunately, they met with a serious carriage accident, owing to the roughness of the road, caused by the breaking up of the frost.

In order to secure a good seat in the train going East, it is necessary to make arrangements a few days before starting. Tickets can be obtained at a score of places in the city, and should be got as soon as possible; and in order to save all unnecessary trouble with the luggage during the journey, sufficient for use in travelling should be separately packed, and the remainder handed over to the Baggage Master, who has an office in the hotel, and who will give checks in exchange, and undertake to deliver it at any hotel or railway station in New York, or any other place in the States that may be named. By attending to this overnight, immense trouble is saved, for, if left until the morning of departure, each traveller has to look after his own baggage amid a scene of the wildest confusion, and quite unprotected from the terrible heat and dust. It was with a sense of great relief that we began to move out of the station, and to feel that at last we were fairly started on our ride across the Rocky Mountains. The railway ride for the first two hundred and fifty miles is a splendid one, through the magnificent Sacramento Valley, which I should think is fifteen or twenty miles wide, and is most fertile. Here corn is grown year after year without any manuring being required. In many "cuttings" through which we passed the soil was twenty feet deep. We passed fields hundreds of acres in extent, with nice houses, orchards, and gardens, surrounded by fine oaks and elms, making the country look like a park for a hundred miles. The corn, which in many places was over ten feet high, was fast ripening, and its glorious golden colour was often charmingly varied by immense patches of Marigold, Eschscholtzia, Lupins, and another beautiful flower which we did not recognise, all in full bloom. We also saw our old Tasmanian friend the Eucalyptus (commonly called the Gum Tree), and many of the quaint Doré-like dead Blue Gums, looking white and ghostly.

THE EUCALYPTUS (from a sketch by the Author).

This is a magnificent State. A gentleman remarked to me that when the richness of the soil is exhausted there remains untold mineral wealth below. The people, too, are very energetic, and there is abundance of capital ; so much so that a money-lender travelling in our carriage complained that it is difficult to get fifteen per cent. per annum now when some twelve years ago he could easily obtain five per cent. per month.

Soon after leaving Sacramento the track ascends the mountains and passes through the old gold-diggings so much spoken of thirty years ago. They are visible all around for miles, and some are still being worked.

All the abandoned ones have been re-worked by the Chinese, who have got a great deal out of them. By and by we stopped at a station where there were several dreadful-looking Indians, some with their faces covered with red ochre and with feathers in their hair; others dressed in scarlet blankets, tall white hats, one-legged trousers and mocassins. They all looked very grave and stolid. I did my best to make one old fellow laugh as he stood on the platform with his arms folded, but his face was stony, and he remained steadfast and unmoveable. Their hair is like whalebone, matted and shaggy; their noses and mouths are broad, and the women look uglier than the men. Several of the women were carrying their *papooses* (babies) suspended over their shoulders, with the legs swathed like Neapolitan children. The only occupation of these degraded creatures is begging and stealing.

While we were passing through swampy tracts the large bull-frogs were giving a croaking concert in full chorus, and a rare noise they made.

Soon we began to sight the snow mountains, and by nine o'clock we were right amongst the pine forests and the snow, and very beautiful the scene looked with the moon shining on it all.

Life on board a "Pullman" train is almost more peculiar than life on board ship. My party were fortunate enough to secure a cabin partitioned off from the rest of the carriage ; but the remainder of the sleeping berths have no partitions, being separated merely by curtains. Inexperienced travellers are apt to forget this, and sometimes cause much amusement in consequence. One morning I heard a young lady

complaining to her mamma that she could not find her
stockings, a remark eliciting numerous offers of assistance from all parts of the carriage. A neighbouring
compartment was occupied by a lady and gentleman,
the former of whom was deaf, and with the peculiarity
often observable in deaf people, she imagined everyone
else was deaf as well; the consequence being that there
were no secrets in that cabin. Every carriage has a
negro attendant, whose duty it is to make the beds and
attend to the lavatories, the ladies' and gentlemen's
lavatories being at opposite ends of the carriage.
At half-past nine o'clock Sambo begins to prepare the
beds, and soon after ten almost everyone has retired,
and, as fortunately there are no decks to be paced, sleep
soon comes to the weary. Arrangements are made for
three meals a day, the train stopping at stations convenient for the purpose, and notice being given half-an-
hour before. Half-an-hour is allowed for each meal,
the invariable charge being one dollar. As the train
stops a general stampede is made toward the dining-
room, the position of which is unmistakable, for at
the door stands a negro, with a face devoid of
expression, vigorously sounding a gong. As each
person passes in he pays his dollar, and makes a rush
to the end of the room, where the cook is usually
stationed. And now happy is he who possesses
the Yankee's qualification for a good diner-out, for
unless he has a long arm, a quick eye, and a silent
tongue, he is likely to come off with much less than a
dollar's worth. The experienced traveller, before sitting
down, gathers all the dishes before him, within arm's
length, and then proceeds to attack them *seriatim*, or

sometimes all at once. Indeed, I think a man of naturally generous disposition, would be made utterly selfish by twelve months' travelling on American railroads. As soon as the half-hour has gone, the guard calls out with a shrill, nasal, Yankee twang, "All aboard," and we once more continue our journey.

Happening one day to say to a fellow-passenger that I was from Birmingham, an American gentleman hearing me came across the carriage, and, raising his hat, said: "I *must* shake hands with a man hailing from the city which returns John Bright to Parliament."

The Pacific Railroad is a single track, and, although a wonderful engineering work, is not by any means a substantial or confidence-inspiring line, if judged by English standards. The rails are old and worn, the bridges and viaducts very lightly constructed, and almost always of wood. I observed in several cases that the carriages were actually wider than the viaducts, many of which are open between the rails. It is hardly to be wondered at that awful accidents sometimes occur. The train in which we were travelling narrowly escaped falling into a ravine 120 feet deep. One dark night, after we had all retired to rest, we were awakened by continued whistling and ringing of bells. It was in vain that we inquired of the guards and attendants as to what was going on, for they, like their brethren all the world over, would give no information. One thing, however, they could not hide from us, for we found we were being taken across a viaduct one carriage at a time, and as we crossed we could see lights moving about at a great depth below. On arriving at Omaha, two days later, we found a full report of the occurrence in the papers. It appears that the viaduct had been discovered to be in an unsafe condition, some of its timbers having been partially burnt, and it was a matter of discussion whether we should be allowed to cross at all; it being ultimately determined, as I have said, to take one car over at a time. Ours was the last train that went over, for before daylight the whole structure had fallen with a tremendous crash. The Indians were on the war-path at the time, and it was supposed that the work of destruction was theirs. The railway here runs through some of the most magnificent scenery in the world. Sometimes its course lies through narrow valleys, or cañons, where there is just room for the railway and the river, sometimes through immense pine forests, and then again on a mere shelf cut in the face of the granite mountain, until the point called "Cape Horn" is reached. This is the turning-point between east and west, and soon afterwards the greatest elevation is attained, 8,200 feet. About sixty miles of the more exposed portion of the road is covered with sheds, to protect it from the snow. This result, however, is not attained without considerable discomfort to the passengers, as the carriages become filled with smoke and dust while passing through.

One of the passengers on our train was an old man who had not crossed the country since he went out to the far west some twenty-six years before—long before the railway had been thought of. The party with which he then travelled was so large that it had to be split into detachments for the convenience of pasturage. One night his section was attacked by Indians, who killed several of the party and drove off most of the horses and cattle. The old man had for many years been a trapper in the Indian country and had invested his hard-won earnings in horses which he was taking out west for the purpose of trade, and he was not disposed to lose them all at one fell swoop without making a bold dash for their recovery. His plan of operations was soon settled, and in the evening he set off in pursuit with half-a-dozen picked men, each with his rifle and a good store of ammunition. After some hours they came upon the scent of the Indians, and moving cautiously forward amongst the scrub, presently saw them around their fires busily engaged in dividing the spoils of the morning. The trapper being a first-rate marksman, it was agreed he should do all the firing, while the others loaded and handed up the rifles as fast as required. Every shot told, and the redskins, judging from the rapid firing that the whole party of white men were upon them, made a regular stampede, leaving horses, and cattle, and other spoil behind them. So, painfully marching on, they came at last to the Mormon settlement and on to the Salt Lake City, where they were subjected to the most cruel treatment at the hands of the " Saints." These people told the travellers it was impossible to get to California by the route they were taking, as the country was swarming with hostile Indians, and they undertook to show them a better way by which they would get there in fifteen days. Many suspected treachery, and a consultation was held, which came to no definite conclusion, except in the case of one man, who, in the heat of debate, was shot dead. It was ultimately decided to adopt the

Mormon advice, and as the route did not admit of wagons, they tried to sell them to the "Saints," who, of course, would not buy, knowing they would have them for nothing before long. Many of the travellers burnt their wagons and harness rather than that the Mormons should have them, but the majority abandoned theirs, and set out without them. Instead of fifteen days the journey took thirty-nine, and only a few survived it, most of the party dying by the way, either by the hand of the Indians or from fatigue.

For about a thousand miles the railway is open to the prairie, the consequence being that frequent accidents occur through cattle straying upon the track. I counted more than twenty carcases of these unfortunates in one day, and on one occasion, while sitting on the steps of the Pullman car, I felt a sudden check, and immediately after the body of a cow flew past. The herds are looked after by men with lassoes, riding very fleet horses. American railroads being much less protected from stray animals than those in England, the locomotives are provided with an apparatus called a "cow-catcher," which consists of an iron framework projecting in front and inclined downwards as near to the rails as possible. The contrivance is successful in moving most living obstacles from the track. For instance, when a cow gets between the rails and sees the train approaching, it becomes dazed, and the iron frame striking the lower portion of the legs takes it up readily. But with a bull it is quite different: when his lordship sees his enemy approaching he puts his chin down upon his fore-feet and waits the onset with a confidence not by any means always misplaced, for in this position his head and feet form a wedge which, becoming inserted beneath the iron frame, frequently throws the engine back upon the train, causing serious accidents. When at Ogden I saw the remains of a goods train which had been wrecked in this way a week before, the engine drivers being killed, also two stow-aways, or "dead-heads," as the Yankees call them, who had secreted themselves under one of the carriages.

SALT LAKE.

Waking one morning we found ourselves in a most awfully desolate country, with scarcely a sign of vegetation—a veritable dry and thirsty land, through which we travelled all day. Towards evening we came to the alkali country, and the plains looked as though they were covered with snow. This is a fearful place, where, before the construction of the railway, many poor emigrants have lain down to die. Soon after, we skirted the margin of the Great Salt Lake and entered Brigham Young's dominions, passing his first town, "Corinné." This town was founded by the Gentiles after Brigham turned them out of the Salt Lake City, but he soon drove them farther off.

We left the train at Ogden in order to pay a short visit to the Salt Lake City, which is situated thirty-six miles off, and is approached by a railway belonging to the Saints. For beauty of situation Salt Lake City is almost unrivalled. It lies in a basin more than twenty miles in diameter, and is surrounded by mountains, some of which are 12,000 feet high, and most of them covered with perpetual snow. At the time of our visit the fruit-trees were in full bloom, and, as each house is surrounded by its garden, the city occupies a large extent of ground, presenting a beautiful appearance from the United States camp, which stands on an elevation commanding the whole city, about two miles off. A portion of the old mud wall, about ten feet high, built by the Mormons to resist the attack of the Indians, still remains standing. Several of the houses are exceedingly well built, and the gardens kept in excellent order; one in particular I was much struck with, and remarked to our guide that it was the brightest and best kept place I had seen since leaving England. He told me it belonged to an Englishman who had left for his native country on the previous day. Curiously enough, when I returned home, I found this man was a brother of my butcher, and was then on a visit home. We observed two ladies sitting in the front of the house engaged in needlework, and were told that they were the two wives of the English Mormon. It was very noticeable that these ladies sat at a considerable distance apart, cordiality (unless it be of hatred) not being a characteristic of these Mormon wives in their relations with each other. At the time of our visit the "Prophet" was down south, looking out for a new location for the Saints, in view of the threatened difficulties with the Central Government. We visited the Tabernacle, and saw the preparations for the new temple, to which the deluded of all nations continue to contribute, although it is exceedingly doubtful that the building will be carried to completion. The man who showed us over the Tabernacle used to work in a London factory; but he told us with a curious twinkle in his eye that the "new job" paid him much the best. At a short distance from the city there is a sulphur spring, of considerable volume, proceeding from the side of the mountains; the temperature of the water is such that eggs can be boiled in it. We slept at Ogden that night in order to be in good time for securing places in the train going east in the morning. When the hotel bill was presented I tendered English gold in payment, having disposed of my U.S. currency. The landlord refused to take it, saying, "He would not have the —— British gold." I explained to him that I had no other money, but to no purpose, so, as the train was almost due, I told him I would pay him when I came that way again, but was not sure when that would be. He quietly said, "I guess I'll take your gold," much to the amusement of the bystanders. At the station here is a printed notice cautioning travellers to "BEWARE OF BOGUS TICKET SELLERS."

For three days after leaving Ogden we travelled through the snow, passing through a series of cañons or gorges, which narrow at the base until there is just room for the brawling stream which runs along the bottom. The railway in such cases is either excavated on one side of the gorge or carried on trestles over the stream. The rocks on the mountain sides, mostly of red sandstone, are very bold and of strange shapes. Amongst them is a very weird-looking group called "'The Witches." Another group, known as "The Buttes," bears a most striking resemblance to a line of strong fortifications commanding the valley. We saw

MONUMENT ROCK.

these at sunset, and the effect of the evening light upon the red sandstone was very fine. In the same neighbourhood is the celebrated Devil's Slide; it is formed by the earth being gradually washed away from between two lines of vertical strata about 20ft. apart. It is some hundreds of feet in length, and descends into the river. This valley was the route taken by the Western Pioneers, and is marked here and there by solitary graves with crosses at their heads.

THE DEVIL'S SLIDE.

The whole 8,000 feet descent from the summit to the eastern plains is made in about four hours. The steam is turned off, the breaks turned on, and down we go. As we were preparing to descend I remarked to the negro attendant that I supposed we must trust the engineer now? "No, sah," said Sambo, "I guess we must trust de ole man up above," pointing to the skies.

CHAPTER IX.

ON reaching Chicago we left "the overland train," with the object of paying a short visit to Niagara. The last stage of our long ride was from Omaha, during which we crossed the Missouri and Mississippi. There being three competing lines to Chicago the pace became greatly accelerated, so much so that during a considerable portion of the long ride it was almost impossible to stand on one's feet, and the country being very dry, the train was enveloped in a cloud of dust almost the whole of the way. We had, however, one compensation, for attached to the train was a well-appointed dining-car, with first-rate *cuisine*. The viands were of the choicest quality, and in great variety. Moreover, the speed of the train was slackened during meals, an arrangement affording a degree of comfort unknown on the Pacific Line. The bill of fare is a curiosity in its way, being garnished with appetising mottoes and sentiments, such as, "As you journey through life live by the way," "Eat and be satisfied," and concluding with an expression of belief that passengers would appreciate this new feature of "Life on the Road."

In going through Chicago we were much surprised by the fine and substantial-looking buildings in every part of the city. There are fifty to one hundred streets, any one of which is equal to the best in London; indeed, it struck me as being more of a city than any place I had ever been in. We observed a whole block of buildings, including a bank on the ground floor, and offices above, being removed bodily without any disturbance of the business operations going on in it. The water for the city supply is taken from Lake Michigan through a pipe which extends two miles into the lake. The capacity of the pumping engines is seventy-five millions of gallons per day, the greatest demand being forty-five millions. During the last few years there have been many disastrous fires in Chicago, directly traceable to the general employment of timber not only in buildings, but for the side walks and roadways. The broad streets referred to above are, however, constructed of a fine warm-coloured sandstone, and all the new streets are being made of the same material. Nevertheless, a considerable number of timber houses remain, constituting a standing danger to the city. While in Chicago I found my passport useful. On going to the bank to get some money on my Letter of Credit the manager told me they had not received a copy of my signature from the bank in England, and that in its absence they could not honour my draft. It was in vain that I showed him my watch and other articles having my name engraved upon them. He looked at them as though he thought there were various ways of getting possession of such articles. I told him I regretted I had not been born with my name on my person, but I was not accountable for the omission. I then thought of my passport, and although he appeared to think that it was possible to obtain possession of that improperly, he accepted it with the remark that "even that is not conclusive," for it should have had a description of my person. We stayed at the Grand Pacific Hotel, which formed a great contrast to the Palace Hotel at San Francisco, being uncomfortable and badly administered.

At Detroit we cross the frontier into Canada, travelling over the Great Western Railway to Niagara. This line was constructed by English contractors, and the superiority of the work is manifested in the smooth, steady motion of the carriages. Compared with the lines we had previously traversed this was most comfortable. We pass through London, Paris, and other places with equally celebrated names, greatly enjoying the forest scenery, numerous clearings and bright little homesteads dotted over the country; and for the first time since leaving England seeing lovely green fields such as we have at home. At Niagara we stopped at the famous Clifton House, where we were joined by friends from England.

Our impressions of Niagara were those common to most visitors—first, a feeling of disappointment, soon succeeded, however, by an ever-increasing sense of the immensity and magnificence of the Falls, which grows upon one the more one sees them.

A sentiment of disgust, however, is inspired by the ruthless desecration of the most beautiful spots by Yankee manufacturers, who have chosen such picturesque positions for their smoky factories. Another annoyance constantly experienced is from the peripatetic

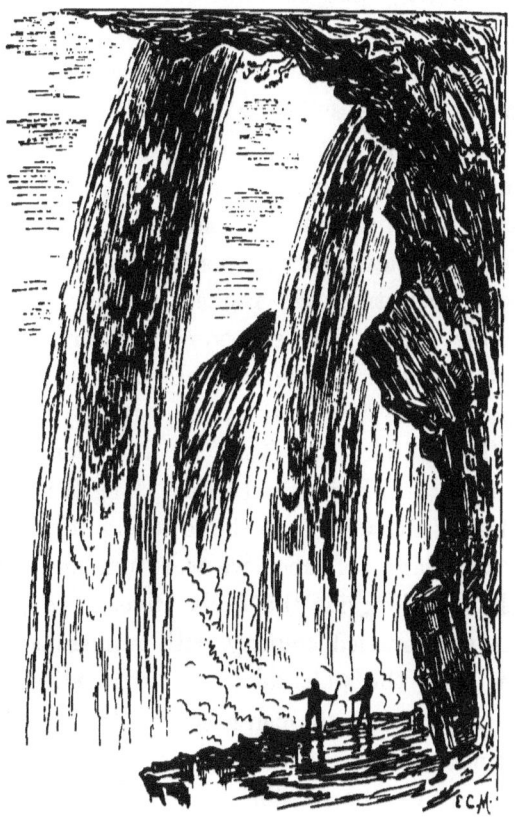

UNDER THE FALLS, NIAGARA.

photographer, who endeavours to persuade you that you are greater than the "Falls." The Falls, indeed, are made to seem a mere background to your photograph, in which he is careful to show you nearest the camera, and hence proportionately by far the most imposing object.

To get into Canada we have to cross the suspension bridge. Going over one day we purchased about £1 worth of photographs of Canadian scenery. On returning with them we were accosted by the American customs officer, who mulcted us in nearly twenty shillings duty. On entering his office to obtain a receipt we observed a "six-shooter" at his right hand, presumably for the purpose of persuasion. On leaving the place I met an American policeman and told him what a shabby transaction it was for the representatives of so great a country. He replied that he guessed the officer must raise his salary. I refrain from any attempt to describe the mighty Falls of Niagara.

On our way to New York we travelled by railway to Albany, the capital of the State of New York, passing through Syracuse, Rome, and Utica, along the shores of Lake Ontario, although from the lowering of the ground and the abundance of trees we were unable to see the lake; thence alongside the Falls River, through very charmingly diversified country with numerous valleys going up from the waterside, well-timbered, and here and there a clearing with open green fields. The houses are in most cases mean-looking plank erections, presenting a very weather-beaten appearance, some painted a very dark red colour. In the evening we reached Albany, an old Dutch town of over two hundred years, and very Dutch-looking it is with its queer red-brick houses, wooden pavements, and trees along the streets, and frequent peeps of the river here and there. Amongst the finest public buildings are those devoted to the national schools, a true gauge of the importance the citizens attach to the education of the people. On our way to New York we had an opportunity of taking a day's sail on the River Hudson in one of the celebrated American river-boats. Going on board we found ourselves on a veritable floating palace. The steamer was a three-decker, two of the decks being covered with splendid carpets, and fitted with arm-chairs of a most comfortable pattern, and with velvet-covered ottomans and couches in all directions. Taking up one of the books from the well-stocked bookstall I saw it purported to be one of a series of standard works by American authors, and on looking down the list I observed the names of Tennyson, Barry Cornwall, and others. Our American cousins were always great at annexation, and the only wonder is they do not call their mother tongue the " American language."

The Americans seem anxious that everyone shall admit that the Hudson is finer than any other river in the world. I have been down the Elbe, through the Saxon Switzerland, also down the Danube and the Rhine. The Hudson is far more beautiful than the Rhine. The banks are thickly wooded, and the villages and country houses prettily situated. It is true that the Hudson lacks the romantic associations of the Rhine, but even in this respect it is not altogether wanting, for does it not possess the Catskill Mountains, with their legend of Rip Van Winkle? But I like the Danube best; its banks are loftier and more rugged, and are covered with pines, and from its comparative narrowness one can see both sides at once. Then again, the ancient towns and monasteries jutting out on the spits of land are infinitely more interesting than the wooden houses along the Hudson. Again, the Elbe, especially in the Saxon Switzerland, is decidedly more

The Pallisades, Hudson River.

beautiful than the Hudson; but for all this the latter is a river of which a nation may well be proud, and we greatly enjoyed our sail upon it.

On a subsequent visit to the Hudson we landed at West Point, the seat of the celebrated military academy founded by Washington, where there are some hundreds of students. Our hotel was situated about two miles from the academy, and overlooked the river from an eminence of about two hundred feet. The river can be seen for some miles winding between steep banks on both sides. The morning after our arrival was a Sunday, and the church bells were ringing for service. There are two opposition churches here, but I have reason to believe they are very charitable to one another; at all events their respective bell-ringers do not believe in the jarring of the sects, for I notice that first one rings out one—two—three—four; then a decent pause, and his neighbour likewise rings out one—two—three—four, and so the celestial harmonies are not disturbed.

On the opposite bank of the river is a place historic in the annals of the Revolution, for here it was that the American General Arnold was stationed while he was carrying on his treasonable correspondence with the ill-fated Major André. Arnold was sitting at breakfast with his officers and some guests when word was brought him that André was captured as a spy by the Americans. Knowing he would surely be incriminated, Arnold pretended he was wanted below on urgent business, and, going down to Beverley landing, he ordered his men to row him to the British man-of-war lying in the river. Poor André, it will be remembered, was hanged by order of Washington. His bust was placed in Westminster Abbey; three times since then has it been mutilated by miscreants. Walking through the village we observed a mean-looking tumble-down tenement, with an equally mean-looking signboard stuck upon it, bearing this inscription:—" John Scales, Justice of the Peace, Notary Public." His " Honour" was sitting inside, in his shirt-sleeves, with a white apron on, while behind him on a shelf were a few old dry-as-dust books, of the law I suppose. The whole place looked totally at variance with our ideas of the majesty of the law; indeed it suggested that "justice"

JOHN SCALES, JUSTICE OF THE PEACE.
(From a sketch by G. T.)

could be had for the buying, and that no one was expected to pay much regard to the decision of such a court. On returning to the hotel I spoke of this functionary to the negro waiter, suggesting that he *dealt in* justice, " Yes, sah; I guess a dollar will go a long way with him," replied he.

Ascending the mountain we came across an old man at work on the roads. He was a German, having come to America in 1841. He served in the Mexican war, and one of his sons was killed in the war against the Southern rebels. The old man said it was hard work mending roads, and that the winters were very severe, "but," said he, "it is a free country, and that makes up for all. In Germany a man dares not open his mouth, but here one can say what one likes."

Passing by a farmyard our curiosity was aroused by seeing the stock of poultry secured by the leg to the fence. As we had often heard in our travels in the States that this was "a great country," we presume this was an expedient adopted to prevent the fowls straying and being lost. Of course, England being so small, such precautions are not necessary.

We returned to New York in another of the celebrated river-boats.

During my stay in the States there were two great subjects which monopolised public attention. These were the Centennial Exhibition which had just been opened: and the wave of corruption among officials and others which was sweeping over the land. More space was occupied in the Press by charges of malversation and fraud on the part of the officials, from the President down to the lowest civil service clerks, and from them through all grades of society, than with the Exhibition itself or with any other subject, while the talk in the streets seemed to be about nothing else. In alluding to the unlawful gains made in this way by many prominent citizens, a New York paper made use of a sentiment of Mark Twain to the effect that whereas in times past folks used to say "poor but honest," now-a-days when you see a rich man who has accumulated money in a proper way it is said that he is "*rich* but honest."

I have travelled in many countries, but in almost everything have found America twice as dear as any other country. The charges are simply monstrous. Having to go from an hotel to the steam wharf, we were not permitted to take our very modest amount of luggage in the omnibus with us, although we had the vehicle all to ourselves; but the hotel people insisted upon sending it in a special wagon, charging two dollars for what a cabman in Birmingham would willingly have done for a shilling. On board the steamer we were charged six shillings each for a plain dinner, without wine, which in England would not have cost more than 1s. 6d. Bound books are equally dear. Pocket volumes, containing not more than one-sixth of the matter in a shilling volume of Chambers' "Miscellany of Entertaining Tracts," were charged two shillings each. Most of the newspapers, also, are very inferior to, yet much dearer than, the English papers. Another form of extortion is to be found in the impossibility, in many hotels, of obtaining information as to the sailing of river-boats, departure of trains, etc., the only apparent explanation being a desire to give "touts" and "loungers," of whom there are many, opportunities of extorting money. These fellows seem to know nothing unless they can hear the dollars chink, or see the dirty greenbacks (and some of them are very dirty). A fellow once gave me in change a dollar note which was so filthy that scarcely a word was legible upon it. It looked as though it might contain smallpox or typhoid, so I asked him to wash it. He said he guessed he would — *for a dollar.*

Against all this, I am bound to say that the charges made by the steamboat companies and most of the railways are exceedingly moderate, and their arrangements in connection with baggage most convenient. On arriving at any of the large cities by river-boat, the agent of the Luggage Express Company comes on board and takes possession of your baggage, giving vouchers for it. He also undertakes to collect any baggage you may have sent to the City Railway Station from distant parts of the country, and very soon after you arrive at your hotel it is brought to you. At the landing stages in such cities as New York there are numbers of cabs, mostly driven by Irishmen, and when they find you have disposed of your luggage and do not require their services, they give vent to their disgust in no measured terms, and if the traveller is a Britisher, he is soon reminded of the fact.

The mode of dealing with baggage on the railway is almost equally convenient. The following will give some idea of it. You are travelling, say, from Aberdeen to Penzance, intending ultimately to proceed by way of London to Dover, and do not require the bulk of your luggage till you arrive at the latter place. On leaving Aberdeen, the Baggage Master takes your superfluous luggage, putting brass labels upon it, thus—

ABERDEEN—DOVER.
846.

giving you corresponding labels, after which you have no further occasion to trouble yourself in the matter until you get to Dover.

We visited the Centennial Exhibition at Philadelphia for the purpose of inspecting the various productions corresponding to our own, hoping, indeed expecting, to find something which would repay us for coming. We were, indeed, repaid, but in a sense totally opposed to what we expected, for we found that so far from Americans being in advance of the English, they were, in many cases, taking credit for so-called "improvements" (claiming them as novelties), which we had been familiar with, and had used in our own works many years before. They appear to be strangely unaware of what has been done in European countries, and a single instance will illustrate this. The machinery in the Exhibition was driven by a single large steam-engine. The newspapers made a great deal of this engine, declaring that it was the largest in the world, and that it had been made in the smallest State—Rhode Island. An American engineer with evident pride took us to see the big engine, which, after all, had a cylinder of only 70in. diameter. We told him that five-and-twenty years before a small engineering firm in Cornwall, England, had made several engines with cylinders 144in. in diameter, and which are yet at work.

We were permitted to inspect some of the most important engineering establishments, and found the tools of such an inferior character that our only wonder was that they could produce either good or cheap work. In most cases the floors of the workshops were inches deep in ferruginous dust. Under such conditions every time a heavy casting is dropped on the floor a cloud of dust must rise, and entering the bearings of the tools, cut them up badly. We found many of the tools actually wedged up because of this.

An American manufacturer speaking to me of a visit he had paid to the Exhibition in company with his foreman, told me how astonished the latter was at the excellence of the European exhibits. He said he had no idea they could make the things half so well, "for," he said, "they are almost as good as ours," and, I added, "only one half the cost."

The agricultural machinery was exhibited in a separate building erected specially for its reception, and here the Americans were unmistakably far ahead of all competitors.

At the time of our visit several consignments of calicoes had been made to England and to various British markets, and sold at prices considerably below what they could be produced at by English manufacturers. This incursion occasioned great disquietude in England until the cause was manifested—viz., over-production. On this point I read an article in a New York Protectionist paper intended as an answer to the Free Trade argument, that Protection increased the price of goods. The article stated that this was not so: and to prove its position said that the tendency of Protection was to induce people to go into manufacturing who know little or nothing of the processes they were undertaking, but who fancy that with the tariff of from 40 per cent. to 80 per cent. upon foreign goods, there must necessarily be a sufficient margin to compensate for mistakes caused by their inexperience. "And so it happens," continues the writer, "that there is great over-production, ruinous competition among American manufacturers, frequent failures, and consequently large stocks of goods are forced on the markets at a great loss, the public getting cheap supplies in consequence." Adam Smith would scarcely have quoted this as one of the methods of adding to the wealth of nations. But if the people at large obtain their cotton goods cheaper through this system of over-production, it is clear that the millowners are not the only sufferers, for it appears from a speech delivered by Mr. Shearman of New York, at the Cobden Club dinner in the present year (1883), that the wages of the factory operatives are twenty per cent. less than in Lancashire, while their hours of labour are from eighteen to twenty per cent. longer.

During the late Fair Trade agitation its advocates were never tired of telling the English working-classes that under Protection their brethren in America were prospering in a remarkable degree, but in the speech to which I have referred Mr. Shearman shows that the average wages in protected trades are actually less than in 1860, the last year of comparative Free Trade, and that while in the ten years previous, wages were constantly increasing, during the succeeding twenty years (1860-1880) there was no appreciable advance, while during the past three years they have been steadily declining; so that here we have one of the staple trades of the country requiring longer hours of labour from the operatives, at considerably lower wages than for the same class in England, while the cost of living is much higher than in this country, and the climate much more trying from the extremes of heat and cold.

Nor is this all, for the American operatives have very much less relaxation than the same class in England, their holidays being very much fewer. Last year my workpeople, in addition to fifty-two Saturday afternoons, had nineteen whole days, although there was abundance of work for them, and the necessities of the business only required six days closing of the works. The English artisan loves to have a deal of liberty, and his earnings enable him to indulge his desire in that respect.

As may be supposed, the ranks of the operatives in the cotton mills of America receive no accession from England, but only from Germany and Scandinavia, where wages are low, and the oppressive military systems drive people from their native countries.

During the last seven years of depression in trade in England it is well known that, taken as a whole, the working classes have suffered comparatively little, the loss falling mainly upon manufacturers, whose profits have been greatly lessened. But how would the working-classes have fared if, in addition to the loss of home trade involved in the failure of the crops for so many years, the same causes were in operation which make it impossible for America to have a great foreign trade?

It is manifest that so long as Protection exists in the United States exports must necessarily be confined almost entirely to such commodities as other countries cannot produce. Until recently the home demand has kept the manufacturers in the States well employed; but competition has now become exceedingly fierce, and they are beginning to tread upon each other's heels. It is this state of things which is destined to exert the most potent influence upon the fate of Protection. The very class which has hitherto been loudest in demanding prohibitory duties upon imports, will soon, from sheer necessity, be found demanding their removal.

It is worthy of note, too, that while under Protection the earnings of the producing class have been steadily declining, colossal fortunes, amounting in one case to twenty or thirty millions sterling, have been built up by individual monopolists. On the other hand, during the same period and under Free Trade, there has been a wider distribution of material comfort in England, and, as shown by the official returns, a decided decrease in the number of millionaires.

In passing through America on my return from Australia in 1876, I expressed the opinion that Free Trade there would be by no means an unmixed blessing for English manufacturers, for whereas at the present time a vessel going to Australia from the United States with a cargo of goods has to come back in ballast, doubling the cost of freight, under Free Trade it would take back a cargo of wool, and the Americans would consequently become our competitors both in buying and selling.

With the single exception of having higher wages—and this advantage is more than balanced by the extra cost of living—I have failed to find that American artisans are in any way better off than the English, while, as I have already shown, their hours of labour are longer and the effect of the climate much more exhausting.

A very striking feature to be met with in most American cities and towns is the large number of tolerably respectable-looking men loafing about and doing nothing. In England such men, only in shabbier dress, would be called "cadgers." I am told there are large numbers who prefer any shifty mode of obtaining a living so long as they can wear a black coat and avoid honest labour. In the villages along the banks of the Hudson I saw more children without shoes and stockings than are to be met with in any part of England in a similar area. They go to school shoeless, and a woman told me that when shoes were put on their feet on Sundays they complained loudly. A land of freedom for tongue and foot!

During the Southern rebellion fears were expressed that the result of emancipation would be to flood the markets of the North with negro labour, but this does not appear to have been the case. As long as slavery existed the North was attractive to the negro as the land of freedom, but when freedom was proclaimed throughout the States the negro naturally elected to remain where he had always been—the climate and surroundings being well suited to him. The head waiter at our hotel at West Point was a slave in Richmond until the middle of the war, when he escaped to Washington. I asked him how he got there. "Oh, by the underground railway," said he. It took him a week to travel the hundred miles, and he had many narrow escapes, but was fortunate enough to come out all right and to get a situation to wait upon one of Abraham Lincoln's sons. He told me his owner, a lady, taught him to read and write in face of the certainty of being sent to jail in case of being discovered. His father was sold away down south sixteen years before, but since that day they had again met at Richmond. "Well," I said, "neither Jeff. Davis nor any of his crew will ever play you such pranks again." "No *Sir*," said he.

The regulation of the liquor traffic in the American cities appears to present as many difficulties as it does in England, especially as regards the Sunday traffic. The Sunday before we left New York the police made a raid upon the liquor dealers in the city, and arrested a number of them for selling during prohibited hours. Their organs threatened all sorts of reprisals at the coming election, and a meeting of the trade was called to condemn the action of the authorities. Most of the requisitionists—judging by their names—were either German or Irish. At the time appointed some hundreds of liquor dealers assembled, and presently a gentleman came on the platform and began to address them. Soon, however, it began to dawn upon the trade that they had been somewhat considerably sold, for the speaker gave them a regular teetotal lecture, enlarging upon the evils the dealers were responsible for, and warning them to forsake their wicked ways. The audience could not stand this, and threatened the orator that if he didn't "make tracks right away" they would give him "something hot," upon which he quietly retired, having given them the first temperance lecture they had ever heard.

Our visit to America was brought to a fitting termination by another glorious excursion on the Hudson: after which it was with great pleasure and satisfaction that we went on board one of the splendid White Star Liners, soon to land again on the shores of dear old England.

EGYPT.

CHAPTER X.

E arrived off Suez about four o'clock on the morning of the 1st of March, having travelled from Australia in the magnificent steamship "Orient." After saying farewell to our friends, at seven o'clock we set out for the shore, our boat being manned by a picturesque party of Arabs. We had about four miles to go, the latter portion of the journey being through water so shallow that the men had to propel the boat by nimbly running forward and placing one end of the oar in the mud and pushing against the other with the shoulder; singing a monotonous song all the while. On arriving at our landing-place opposite the Custom House, a motley crowd rushed forward, some dressed in night-shirts, some in towels, others in their own black skins only. When we stopped, a score of them dashed into the water and began to seize our luggage, seeing which our boatmen called to us to beat them on the head with our umbrellas, and to kick them off; but we

managed to defend our property by loud words, which broke no bones. Then we were carried ashore amidst such shrieking, hustling, jostling, and shouting as I had never heard or seen before. The luggage was set down in the middle of the square to await the arrival of an official from the Custom House. After a very slight examination we were permitted to pass, and then began another battle for the luggage; but we

A Dragoman.

selected as our dragoman a tall, stout fellow named Hassan, who quickly routed the others; and then a file of these half-naked Arabs marched off to the hotel with the luggage on their backs. The Suez Hotel is a very comfortable establishment, with large, clean, and airy rooms, and bright and attentive native servants.

After breakfast we went for a stroll through the town. The streets are very narrow, and the tiny shops are filled with vegetables and other garden produce, oils, simple metal wares, etc. In one street the Bedouin Arabs have stalls for the sale of charcoal, brought by them from the desert; a very sullen, repulsive set of fellows they appear to be. There are few European buildings, and what there are were built for the French officials during the construction of the Canal. These were all vacated during the Franco-German war, and very few French have since returned, consequently the houses are in a very dilapidated condition.

Before leaving England we had arranged for a party of our friends to meet us at Suez, and on returning from our stroll in the town, we walked for a while in the large inner court of the hotel, when presently we saw our friends entering, they having landed just three hours after our arrival from Australia.

After lunch, nine of us took donkeys and had a ride round the town and neighbourhood. Not being assured of my riding ability, I asked my companions to keep near me, which they promised to do, and which they doubtless would have done if they could; but alas! their noble brutes dashed off at full speed, and I was left alone. At every street corner stood a mob of darkies shouting, laughing, and begging, and calling out the names of the various donkeys, "Mrs. Langtry," "Mrs. Cornwallis West" (this was mine), "Mr. Spurgeon," etc. On getting back to the hotel gates there was a crowd of about fifty donkeys, all their fifty drivers wanting us to engage them for our next ride, and it required a vigorous use of Hassan's stick to clear a passage for us.

On the following morning we left for Cairo by train, and in due time Hassan appeared with about a dozen men and a shaky old wagon to take our luggage to the station, and truly it was a formidable lot— a lady and gentleman from Australia having no less than nine trunks. At the hotel gate stood the usual fifty donkeys,

An Egyptian Donkey-boy.

their drivers all shrieking out to you to take their donkeys. "My donkey good donkey, sah; his name, Mrs. Langtry." "'Dis donkey, Sir Roggar (sic) Tichborne, sah; he go gentle." You have to push through the crowd of men and animals as you best can. The never-ceasing word *backsheesh*, or its abbreviation *'sheesh*, hissing in your ear all the way. On suddenly turning a corner you may come upon a lot of children or grown-up people engaged in play or other occupation, but they are always ready. Their hands are immediately stretched out, and the cry is on their lips, *'sheesh!* *'sheesh!* nor do they seem surprised if you fail to respond. Sometimes I vary it by putting out my own hand, with temporary success as far as checking their begging goes, but they are soon equal to the occasion, and with mock gravity will offer a quarter piastre— about a halfpenny—and then you laugh and they laugh.

I had often read, that properly to understand Biblical allusions it is necessary to travel in the East. This constant extending of the hand for *backsheesh* gave me an entirely new appreciation of the passage, "Ethiopia shall yet stretch forth her hand."

After much excitement the train at last starts, and a mob accompanies it as far as they can keep up by running, hoping against hope that you will at length relent and throw them some money. Once I offered a beggar a new penny, but he handed it back very gravely, saying "No good—piastre" (meaning that he wanted a piastre); but I pretended to be offended, and did not give him anything.

Every little station on the road is infested with crowds of natives hoping for *backsheesh*, and it is wonderful what vast numbers of people there are who have nothing to do. At most stations you will see an ill-favoured fellow with a goat-skin across his back, filled with water, but I should have to be very thirsty indeed before I could drink from it. An hour after leaving Suez we saw our old friend the s.s. Orient in the Canal close alongside, having taken twenty-four hours to accomplish this distance.

THE S.S. "ORIENT."

At Ismaïlia we stopped some time, and a lad wanted to clean my boots, which, however, did not require cleaning, so I told him to black the bare feet of a brown boy who was standing by. This he proceeded to do in the presence of a crowd of grinning spectators of all colours—yellow, brown, coffee-coloured, and jet black. The lad whose feet were blacked seemed to enjoy the fun very much, and when it was over appeared to think he was entitled to a half piastre as well as the operator, so he got it. The shoeblack then brought an ebony Nubian, whose skin was already a shining black. He asked me if he might do his feet, but I made him understand it was quite unnecessary. A grave-looking Turk observing the proceedings gave a look which seemed to say, "Mad English again."

At Zagazig we stayed two hours for luncheon, and were much interested with the infinite variety of costume and feature among the crowds thronging the station. About half an hour before reaching Cairo, on looking through the window, we had our first view of the Pyramids. On our arrival at Cairo we were greeted with a chorus of the usual kind, but having "wired" to the hotel a porter was awaiting us with an omnibus, and we were soon comfortably located in the new Grand Hotel.

A walk to the Nile Bridge gave us a good view of the river. The road to the Pyramids passes for some distance through a fine avenue of trees, and the river having encroached on the soil too near to the roots, we saw for the first time a phase of Egyptian life which is not pleasant—viz., forced labour. About 1,500 men were engaged in piling up earth against the roots, forming a thick, deep embankment against the river. The soil is carried in baskets, and from the elevation where we stood the men looked like a swarm of ants. These men are provided by the Sheiks of the villages on the demand of the Government, who pay nothing whatever for the labour. The men receive neither wages nor food, but each village looks after the families of its absentees, and attends to their work until their return. The men certainly seemed to labour with a will.

The Nile begins to rise about the end of June, reaching its greatest height about the end of September, continuing for about fifteen days at twenty-four feet above low-water level. If the rise be thirty feet great damage is done, and if it fail to reach eighteen feet famine ensues.

We rode for some distance along the valley of the Nile, which varies from two to twelve miles in width. It is very fertile, the soil being more than forty feet deep. It is only needful to sow the seed immediately after the inundation, and in about four months the harvest is ready to be gathered. The plough in use is a very primitive article; but the looseness of the soil renders stronger ploughs unnecessary. In many places as we went along we saw the natives irrigating by means of the bucket and pole, with a counterbalance at the end (*shadouf*), raising water from the Nile and sending it along the channels over the fields. In one field we saw agriculture being carried on as Adam would have done before the Fall, had it been necessary, the men being quite naked, and digging the earth with their hands.

Returning to the city we took a walk through old Cairo, along the narrow streets, passing many little workshops where various trades were being carried on, the owners appearing pleased at our noticing them at work. In one place some men were grinding beans with a huge pestle and mortar, and showed us some of the meal. In a secluded corner we saw about a dozen old fellows in every variety of costume sitting on the ground listening to a very animated story being told by one of the party. They appeared to be greatly interested, every now and then lifting up their hands in amazement. These professional story-tellers are a great institution in Cairo.

Passing down one of the narrow streets our attention was arrested by the busy hum of children's voices, which we found proceeded from an upper room, the casement of which was open. Our guide told us it was a school, and that the children were repeating passages from the Koran. One of our party, who had

THE SCHOOLMASTER "ABROAD."

not forgotten the pranks of his boyhood, threw a number of new threepenny pieces into the midst of the boys, causing great excitement and confusion. Presently an old man, with a fringe of white hair encircling his dark face, and wearing a huge pair of brass-framed spectacles, appeared at the open window brandishing his cane at us, but in a moment his whole attitude changed, and holding out his hand he uttered the familiar cry of—*backsheesh*.

A "PEEP."

Our walk took us through one of the bazaars, which consist of very narrow lanes full of shops, with dealers in every variety of goods, most of which are made in the open. We were particularly struck with the beautiful embroideries of gold and silver thread, and the expeditious way in which the workmen executed the various designs. All were very anxious we should buy, and I overheard one old rascal offer our Coptic guide ten per cent. commission on our purchases. We, however, made none. In passing the carpet bazaar we saw an English party buying dingy carpets.

THE JEWELLERS.

The most interesting part of our day's experiences was spent in the manufacturing quarter. There are no large factories in Cairo, and I question if more than half a dozen people are employed at any one place. The work is carried on in the most primitive fashion in the little shops facing the street. There can be but few secrets in the various trades, as the workshops are

"BERY CHEAP, SAH!"

all shallow, and open to the streets. All the jewellers are in one street about 8ft. in width, each of them being provided with a safe, obviously of English manufacture. I do not think, however, that the bellows used by them were made in Birmingham, for it was curious to note that they had no valves. At the end of the jewellers' street sits an old fellow like Abraham or Isaac, weighing precious metals in a pair of evidently very accurate scales. This man acted as general weigher for the trade, and his operations were carried on in the face of the public. Leaving the bazaars we met a crowd of natives gesticulating, shouting, and frolicking in a very excited manner. Standing aside to allow the throng to pass, we found it was a bridal procession conducting a bride to her husband's home. A few tattered minstrels walked in front, making a hideous noise on pipes and drums, while a gang of young men jumped and danced about, and indulged in the wildest horse-play. The women were ornamented with strips of gilt paper and coloured ribbons, and had their cheeks thickly coated with rouge. The bride walked under a canopy consisting of four poles covered with canvas and was quite enclosed. Sometimes this portable tent would collapse upon the fair one, whose struggles were prominently manifested by bulges in the canvas. The whole party seemed to be making the most of the occasion.

We next visited the mosque of Sultan Hassan, which was built in the 14th century, at a cost of £600 per day for the three years it took to complete. It is the finest mosque in Cairo. While standing beside the Sultan's tomb within the mosque our guide related its history. He said that for three years the Sultan had been absent from Egypt on pilgrimages, and that during his absence his Grand Vizier declared himself Sultan. Hassan hearing of this returned to Cairo in the disguise of a poor pilgrim, and finding that he had still many adherents he consulted with some of the principal of them as to the best way of regaining his rights. He first obtained permission to build this mosque, and

THE MOSQUE OF SULTAN HASSAN.

when it was finished his partisans assembled in the building in large numbers. Hassan, still in the pilgrim's habit, rose to preach to the people—this was the preconcerted signal for a general massacre of the usurper and his supporters; and thus Hassan recovered his throne. At the entrance to the mosque our boots were covered with sandals, so that our feet might not touch the holy floor; but custom does not demand the removal of the hat. In the court-yard is a fountain where the faithful perform their ablutions before prayer. In front of the niche looking towards Mecca were about a dozen persons at their devotions. Just in advance of them stood a mollah or priest, and as he bowed his head or kneeled they did the same, concluding with chanting or singing a prayer. Whilst we were looking around a little boy was following us, keeping a sharp look out lest our slippers should come off, and if they showed any signs of coming loose he at once brought up a man to fasten them.

One of the sights of Cairo is the egg-hatching establishment. This institution is rendered necessary, because the hens are too idle to hatch their eggs in this country, consequently the operation has to be artificially performed. The people bring their eggs to the hatching place and receive one chicken for every two eggs. I observed the Egyptian eggs are very small, due also to the laziness of the hens, doubtless.

We next visited the citadel and the mosque of Mohammed Ali, a magnificent pile, built early in this century. In the courtyard of this place the Mamelukes in 1811 were massacred by order of Mohammed Ali.

Fearing their power he invited them to the mosque, and closing the gates slaughtered them all, save one who escaped by leaping with his horse from the parapet. The horse was killed, but the rider was uninjured. About 450 persons were here massacred, and 800 in other parts of the city. The citadel commands a magnificent view of the city and surrounding country, and every evening large parties of tourists assemble there to see the sunset.

The excursion to the Pyramids of Gizeh is now much more easily made since Ismaïl completed the carriage road by way of compliment to our Royal Princes on their visit. Our party was conveyed in carriages, while donkeys had been previously sent forward for the use of the ladies. While on the carriage-road the view of the Pyramids is altogether lost till within a mile of the end of the journey, acacias having been thickly planted on either side of the road. On leaving the carriages we were at once surrounded by beggars, who continued to infest us all the time we were in the neighbourhood. Some were loud, almost menacing in their demands, others soft and insinuating. One kind, which I call the "quiet devil" or "familiar," creeps by your side, and whispers in your ear confidentially that he is "a good man"; that the others are "bad men"; that he will not bother you for anything; that you are "a good man"; that he will "help you, and keep off the others." But alas! he too is sure to whisper in conclusion *backsheesh*. If the road is a little rough these "good men" seem to fancy you cannot get on without help, so one on each side puts a hand under your arm and half carries you along. It is quite useless to

ASCENDING THE GREAT PYRAMID.

protest; they look at you as though they would say, "poor man! he thinks he can walk by himself; but we know better; he would fall at once did we not hold him up." And then, when we reach level ground again, there is a universal chorus of—*'sheesh, backsheesh.*

On arriving at the little house at the foot of the Pyramids our guide Abaid summoned the Sheik of the village, who proceeded to detail two men for each person who intended to make the ascent—ladies and fat men being allotted four men each to help them up. The weather being extremely hot my sister and I were content to see the rest of the party make the ascent while we sat in a shady place at the base. A group of twenty Arabs of the most patriarchal aspect squatted on the ground in front of us in a half-circle; immediately our eyes fell upon any one of them he mutely extended one hand—not so much to help us as to be helped—instantly lowering it without complaint on our looking elsewhere. This would become monotonous. I would occasionally show by my look that I was annoyed, upon which the beggar would get a crack over his head from one of his neighbours.

The Great Pyramid of Cheops is 732ft. along the base line and 460ft. high, covering an area of 586,000 square feet—about equal in extent to Lincoln's Inn Fields in London. Its height is about 60ft. higher than the cross on St. Paul's Cathedral. My wife managed the ascent very well, and also went with the rest to explore the interior, and all seemed greatly pleased with their exploits. A fee of two francs to the Sheik and a franc apiece to the helpers is the regular charge for each person; but even the Sheik is not above taking a little extra by way of *backsheesh*. Our party were quite ready for their lunch, which Abaid quickly spread out in the little house provided by the Government for the accommodation of visitors. We were shown into a large room, and while at table the doorways were filled with a hungry crowd, quarrelling, laughing, and jostling each other. Some of the bolder spirits at length got into the

VIEW ON THE NILE.

room, but our guide seizing his stick administered two or three heavy blows, and soon cleared them out. It was wonderful to see how tamely big men will allow themselves to be driven. Truly the stick is a great institution in Egypt, although perhaps none but the ruling class would acquiesce in the inscription found in one of the ancient tombs to the effect that "The stick came down from heaven—a blessing from God."

Before sitting down to eat, a boy brought water that we might wash our hands. The mode was certainly primitive. We had to hold our hands out of the window while he poured water over them. A noisy crowd of Arabs were sitting under another window, and a barber in the midst was operating upon the head of one of them, and it was really wonderful how cleverly he shaved, making a clean sweep of every lock and every hair. I asked Abaid if the men were under a vow, but he said it was because summer was coming on, and it would be cooler without hair.

THE SPHINX.

After a scene of great confusion in paying the various claimants, during which the Sheik had to make a vigorous use of his long stick, we started to see the Sphinx, which is about 500 yards off. Before leaving,

A WASH AND A SHAVE.

I called the Sheik and gave him two francs, that he might instruct his men to keep the mob from us. This he accepted with great solemnity, and in parting shook hands in a most impressive manner.

The Sphinx is cut out of the solid rock, and is about thirty feet from the top of the head to the bottom of the chin, and about fourteen feet across the face, the body being 140 feet long. I could see no beauty in the face, the features being almost obliterated.

Near the Sphinx is a fine underground temple formed of immense granite blocks and polished alabaster. The pavement is of granite and is perfectly smooth. Some of the finest statues at Bûlak were found in a well adjoining this temple.

Leaving our hotel at seven a.m., we started for Gizeh station *en route* for Sakkara, the railway taking us as far as Bedrashên. We had engaged eleven donkeys for carrying our party and the food necessary for the whole day's refreshment. The confusion at Gizeh station in obtaining our tickets and getting the donkeys into the train was something tremendous. Fortunately, the morning was rather cool.

On arriving at Bedrashên we had some difficulty in finding the right donkeys, and I had great misgivings about the prospective five hours' ride; but at last we got fairly off, and by degrees my confidence returned. We soon reached Mîtrahîneh, the site of ancient Memphis, now only marked by a vast number of heaps and mounds of rubbish, under which are doubtless buried many treasures of ancient Egyptian art. A number of articles which have been recently dug out were shown in a rude enclosure; one or two of the statues beautifully executed. Lying in a pool, face downwards, is a statue of Ramses II., belonging to the British Museum, but the authorities of that institution have not yet taken the trouble to remove it. The statue is 50ft. long, and is of siliceous limestone, very hard, and bearing a high polish. In one hand the figure holds a scroll bearing his name, and at his side is his little daughter, reaching to his knee. The face is still quite smooth, the features are sharply cut and delicately finished, and the expression perfectly preserved, looking really beautiful. Memphis was said by Herodotus to extend for six miles. It was conquered in turns by Persians, Assyrians, and Romans, each of whom did their share towards ruining it, and when at last the Mohammedans conquered the country, its doom was sealed, and the stones of its palace and temples taken away to build the new city of Cairo. The dykes being no longer kept in repair, the overflow of the Nile gradually piled up the mud year by year, and this, with the sand from the desert, has, in the course of ages, made Memphis little more than a name. Memphis is called in the Bible *Noph*, and in the time of the Patriarchs was the capital of Lower Egypt; but the prophecy of Jeremiah, xlvi. 19, has been literally fulfilled: "Noph shall be waste and desolate."

Leaving Memphis we go on to Sakkara, for thousands of years the ancient Necropolis or burying-ground. In the centre stands the great Step Pyramid, built in steps of comparatively small pieces of stone. It is said to be not only the oldest pyramid, but also the most ancient monument of any kind in the world. The cemetery is four and a half miles long by an average of three-fourths of a mile in width, and being full of holes it is necessary to be very careful in crossing it. The ground is strewed with skulls and other human bones, some of the former being of great thickness. Soon we reached the house of Mariette Bey, built for his use when he was engaged in his explorations, and here, by his permission, parties are at liberty to rest and take their lunch.

The first object of interest is the Serapeum, or Apis Mausoleum. When alive, the sacred bull was worshipped in a splendid temple at Memphis, and lodged in an adjoining palace. When dead he was buried in this mausoleum, in a vault excavated out of the solid rock, his body being placed in a huge sarcophagus hewn out of a single piece of granite, and hollowed into a regular square to receive the body. A cover, also of granite, and weighing many tons, was then placed over it. The size of the sarcophagus is 13ft. long, 7ft. 6in. wide, and 11ft. high.

This mausoleum had for ages been known to exist somewhere, but no one knew the locality. The ancient Strabo wrote, " There is also a serapeum in a very sandy spot where drifts of sand are raised by the wind to such a degree that we saw some sphinxes buried up to their heads, and others half covered." Mariette, recollecting this passage, observed in 1860 a sphinx's head appearing through the sand, and it at once occurred to him that this must be the site of the avenue of which mention is made by another ancient writer, so he commenced a clearing and laid bare 141 sphinxes. To do this he had to make a cutting in the sand 70ft. deep; but at length he was rewarded by discovering the entrance to the mausoleum.

There are several galleries for the different dynasties, but only one is now shown, the interments in which date from 650 B.C. down to 50 B.C. The galleries

THE SERAPEUM, SAKKARA.

extend for 400 yards, and there are now twenty-four sarcophagi in their places. Three of these are beautifully sculptured. One of them is of polished granite, and although the engraving is only $\frac{1}{16}$in. deep, a mere scratch in the polish, it is as clear as when first done, over 2,000 years ago, and so perfect is the stone that it rings like a bell when struck.

From the Serapeum we proceeded to examine one of the tombs, also excavated by Mariette Bey. It is called the Tomb of Tih. Over the doorways of these ancient tombs it was the custom to inscribe the name and titles of the deceased, and also an invocation to the God of Tombs (the tomb having been built during life by the person himself), with these objects :—

1st.—To accord to deceased propitious funeral-rites, and a good burial-place after a long and happy life.

2nd.—To be favourably disposed to deceased in his journey beyond the tomb.

3rd.—To secure to him, to all eternity, the proper payment of funeral-offerings by his relations.

A list of these offerings is carved upon the walls, which are covered with sculptures representing the scenes in which the deceased had been engaged during life, ending with a representation of the conveyance of the mummy to the tomb. The tomb itself contains several apartments, in which the relatives met upon certain anniversaries to present votive-offerings, etc.

We were astonished to see the perfect state of preservation in which the tomb remains. The sculptures on the walls are as sharp and clear and the colours apparently as bright as when laid on. Sand is a good preservative when not in motion, and to this must the marvel be ascribed. Over the door is the inscription giving Tih's name, and stating that he was a priest; and on the walls of the first chamber are representations showing statues of Tih being embarked in boats and oxen being brought for sacrifice, one of them being offered up. There is another showing Tih with his wife and family watching his people at work in the farmyard. Some of them are bringing sacks of grain for the poultry; others are fattening the birds by making and forcing pellets of flour down their throats. Behind this there is a view of the farm-buildings, the roofs being supported on carved wooden pillars. In the middle there is a pool where ducks are swimming, while cattle are seen pasturing in the fields around. Among the birds Tih kept are cranes and pigeons, ducks and geese. He had also cattle of every size and kind, including antelopes, gazelles,

FROM THE TOMB OF TIH.

and wild goats. Then come the boats filled with jars and bales transporting farm produce down the Nile. In another place men are shown carrying fruits and vegetables, and pigeons in cages. Farther on are seen men drawing statues enclosed in temples of wood, half-a-dozen dragging with ropes, while one pours water on the road to make it easier. In another room Tih is shown as a sportsman in a boat; in one hand he holds a decoy-bird, while with the other he hurls a curved stick like an Australian boomerang. In the water are seen crocodiles and hippopotami: a crocodile and hippopotamus are fighting, the latter being evidently victorious; some of the servants are trying to catch them, and the hippopotamus is just being hooked with a sort of harpoon. (This scene recalls the verse in Job, "Canst thou draw out the leviathan with a hook?") Here again the fish are being drawn in nets into the boats, while the work of the farm goes vigorously on. Cows are seen crossing a ford and browsing in a field, while herdsmen are driving a flock of goats. Oxen are ploughing just as we saw them in the fields to-day, and with a very similar plough. The seed is being sown, corn reaped, and men with three-pronged forks are gathering it into heaps while the oxen are treading it out. In another place the corn is being tied into sheaves, and donkeys are being brought up with much fuss and use of the stick to take it to the granaries. Some of these scenes are drawn with inimitable humour. Carpenters are engaged in making furniture, and shipwrights in building boats, while Tih is always present directing each operation.

The Egyptians were said by Diodorus to call their houses hostelries, and their tombs their everlasting homes.

We now remounted our donkeys, and for an hour rode over the sandy desert through dreadful mud villages, from which all the population turned out as we passed, crying with all their might—'*sheesh*, '*sheesh*, *backsheesh*, '*sheesh*, '*sheesh*.

Passing several strings of camels—which I described as "camelcades," coining a word for the purpose—we soon regained the delightfully fertile country which is watered by the Nile. For more than two hours we trotted and galloped along through a very rich country, where hundreds of acres of date-palms were growing—where the young corn was waving, and peas, beans, and cucumbers in great luxuriance—no more dust nor sand, but a pleasant breeze and bright sun, with nothing to mar the pleasure except the sight of the wretched natives. Most of the children are absolutely naked, while their parents' clothes are of the most limited description. We halted for lunch under some palm-trees by a branch of the Nile, and then proceeded to the carriages, which we had

A CAMELCADE (sketched by the Author).

ordered to meet us in the Gizeh road. Some of us had to ride back into Cairo on our donkeys, and on our way we passed the Khedive, who cordially acknowledged our salutation. All our party agreed in saying that to-day's excursion was one of the most delightful we had ever had.

PRAYERS IN THE DESERT.

CHAPTER XI.

FRIDAY being the Mohammedan Sabbath we devoted this day to the Dancing and Howling Dervishes, as they hold their principal *zikr* or ceremonial on that day. We first visited the convent of the dancing Dervishes and witnessed one of their performances, and certainly a curious spectacle it was. In the centre of the room a space of about 50ft. in diameter is railed off, and about twenty solemn-looking men in hats like the tall "tile" without brims are sitting opposite the door. They looked like a lot of ancient "Friends" at the head of a meeting. In the gallery above were some musicians, one of whom was playing a flute in a melancholy manner, and another reciting a prayer. At a certain point the Dervishes within the circle bow and rise, and taking off their outer garments begin walking round the enclosure with solemn steps and slow, headed by the Chief Priest or Sheik. On passing the carpet upon which the Sheik has been sitting they turn and bow, and this is repeated two or three times; then they go into the middle of the enclosure, spreading out their garments like ladies in the old minuet; the music quickens, and they begin to whirl around on one foot, occasionally touching the ground with the other. The performers' eyes are closed (or appear to be so), but they keep on in perfect order—never touching one another—while the old Priest walks about among them. Some of the more experienced Dervishes can revolve fifty or sixty times a minute, keeping it up for nearly half an hour. It was a curious proceeding altogether, and, for a wonder, no *backsheesh* was demanded, the Priests being supported by endowments and occasional gifts from the Khedive. Mounting our donkeys we rode off to the Howling Dervishes, where we found them in full howl. About twenty of them were engaged in making the most hideous noise imaginable. These fellows had their hair very long and shaggy, and threw it about their heads in the wildest manner. Every time they raise their heads they utter the word *HU* (God alone), which sounds like the yell of a wild beast, at times the excitement rising to such a height that some of them would foam at the mouth and fall to the ground apparently in a fit. They wound up their proceedings with a prolonged howl and a deep grunt. These Dervishes, like their dancing brethren, are supported by Government endowment.

I have no doubt that when first instituted these "pious orgies" were entered upon with a due sense of solemnity, and I believe in places remote from the regular tourist route the religious feeling still predominates, but the Howling and Dancing Dervishes in Cairo have long since become one of the regular sights to which foreign visitors are always taken.

Upon the occasion of our visit there were several clergymen present, more than one artist, and a number of ladies, amongst the latter being a placid looking Quaker, who, with hands folded before her, was calmly surveying the "creaturely activity" of the Howling enthusiasts.

We afterwards paid a visit to Miss Whately's Schools, at the British Mission. There are over 300 native children here, and we heard many of them read in English and French, and also do some exercises in translation. The girls were engaged in embroidering, reading, and writing, and they sang two hymns in Arabic while we stayed. Then we saw them muster for the recess, and a bright little fellow stepped out into the middle of the hall and repeated the Lord's Prayer, first in English and then in Arabic, after which they went out in a most orderly manner. Miss Whately seems much encouraged at the result of her many years' labours; but I have no doubt she has had her times of discouragement. My wife visited an Arab school in Syria, the superintendent of which told her that after two years' continuous labour amongst the people of his district, the result was so unsatisfactory that he was greatly discouraged and was inclined to abandon the mission. Calling the people together he told them of his disappointment, and said that although he had worked diligently amongst them for so long a time, they appeared to be no better than before, and that he felt that he must leave them. The people, who had received many benefits from him in various ways, began to be seriously alarmed, and entreated him to try them yet again. One man got up in the meeting and said,

"Teacher, you must not go, you have made us much better. When you came first there was a woman living near who used to steal all the fowls in her neighbourhood, but now," he said, "*she only steals the eggs.*" The superintendent's features somewhat relaxed on hearing this, and the quick-witted Arabs immediately perceiving their advantage, renewed their appeals, a woman rising and saying, "Teacher, when you came first my neighbour's son used to thrash his mother every day, but since he has been at your school he only thrashes her once a month." The superintendent remained, and is well satisfied with the progress which has since been made.

In the afternoon we went for a drive in the Shubra Avenue, which is the Rotten Row of Cairo. The custom is to drive quickly up one side, returning slowly on the other, the drive occupying an hour. The Khedive drove past us in his carriage, preceded by two magnificent fellows (*sáis*) whose duty it is to run in front of the carriage. They were dressed in gorgeous gold tissue waistcoats, long white skirts, a silk sash of many colours round the waist, a fez with long tassel, legs and feet bare, and in the hand a handsome staff. These men run quite as fast as the horses, keep up the pace for a couple of hours, and are employed to clear the crowded streets for the carriages. This they do by shouting loudly in a fine resonant voice, which is very effectual. The avenue was crowded with carriages, some of them containing ladies of the harem. Their carriages have windows all round. Some of the ladies are shrouded as for burial; others leave only the eyes uncovered, while some (the prettiest,

A RUNNER, OR *SAIS*.

presumably) wear only thin gauze veils, through which their faces are plainly to be seen. All wear the same languishing expression, and appear to be very fond of peeping at the Europeans, and as we passed and repassed them they would recognise us with a smile, and then, to save appearances, turn away. When we passed the guard-house the soldiers turned out, thinking it was the Khedive's carriage, and drew up in saluting order.

In Shubra Avenue.

They were greatly disgusted on discovering their mistake. At four o'clock a general stampede of carriages, horsemen, runners, and pedestrians takes place, and the road is soon quite deserted.

One of the features of Cairene life is the universal use of donkeys by all classes of the people; ancient women shrouded from head to foot in black gauze, old men with long grey beards, and noses not much shorter—their heads wrapped in turbans, and robes covering the donkeys' backs—jogging along, rubbing against the British tourist, the latter looking anything but grave and serious on his Jerusalem pony. Our party certainly did not look more *bizarre* than others; but we should not feel inclined to enter Birmingham in the same state as we often entered and left Cairo. One morning we got up early for a donkey-

WATER CARRIERS.

ride across the Nile to see, amongst other things, the garden and farm produce arrive from the country round. Crossing the Nile we turned down a fine avenue of sycamores, two or three miles long. The Khedive's gardens lie on one side and the river at the other. Moored to the river bank was an Englishman's *dahabieh* or Nile boat. A party had just returned from the cataracts, and on the upper deck we observed a dead crocodile. Riding by one palace towards another, we passed a crowd of people on their way to market, with bullocks, goats, camels laden with clover, women with the round cakes so common here, and a great variety of other things. Presently we sighted the Pyramids, one side lit up with the morning sun, while another was in deep shadow. The Sphinx was also plainly to be seen.

Leaving the Gizeh Road leading to the Pyramids we turned towards Cairo, our donkeys instantly knowing that we were homeward-bound, and needing no persuasion to gallop back to breakfast. On nearing the bridge we came upon hosts of camels, donkeys, and oxen laden with produce, and being assessed for the octroi or town-tax. The police were armed with long spikes, which they pushed into the load to ascertain if anything else was packed inside. It was an interesting scene—the busy crowd, the magnificent river, and the brilliant morning sunshine making up a picture not easily forgotten.

One of the most interesting drives in the neighbourhood of Cairo is to Heliopolis—part of the way lying through a fine avenue of acacias—and passing the old camping ground used as a *rendezvous* by the Mecca pilgrims. It is the old caravan road, and stretches far away into the desert, from which came to us a delightfully fresh breeze. We also passed the Abbaseyeh Palace, built by Abbas Pasha, who, fearing assassination, lived here in seclusion, keeping sentinels on the towers to give warning of the approach of a mob, and

The Tombs of the Khalifs.

dromedaries and fleet horses always ready saddled for escape into the desert. He was, however, murdered at last in spite of all his precautions.

Along the road are some beautiful plantations of palms, oranges, and lemons, castor-oil and other plants growing in the greatest luxuriance. Heaps of oranges were lying on the ground. After driving through a fine olive plantation we came out upon an extensive plain, where, in 1517, Sultan Selim defeated the last of the Mameluke Dynasty, and made Egypt a Turkish province. Here too, in 1800, the French defeated the Turks and regained possession of Cairo. Our guide called a halt in order to show us a fine old sycamore, called the virgin's tree, under which Joseph and Mary are said to have rested during their flight into Egypt. I asked Abaid if he believed the story. Placing his hand upon his heart and bowing his head, he replied, with something of the sententiousness of a Dr. Johnson, "Sir, I am a Christian!" I felt inclined to tell him that I also was a Christian, but that I did not believe it; but then why should I disturb his honest belief? Soon the obelisk of Heliopolis came in view, and we knew we were near it by the crowd of youngsters swarming round the carriage. But I adopted my old plan of being the first to ask for *backsheesh*, causing them to laugh so heartily that they could hardly take up the cry.

The obelisk is about 6ft. square at the base and about 68ft. high; it is the oldest in Egypt, and was erected by the founder of the twelfth dynasty. The inscriptions on its four sides give its history and the account of its erection about 3,000 B.C.

A Street in Bûlak

Heliopolis was called Bethshemish by the Jews, and in Exodus is called ON. It was here that Joseph married Asenath, the daughter of Potipherah, and where Moses became learned in the wisdom of the Egyptians. Here Plato and Herodotus studied, and Josephus says—" The city was given to the Children of Israel as their residence when they came down into Egypt." The obelisk, as we see it, was old when Abraham came into the country; but, notwithstanding its venerable age and intensely interesting associations, it has not been too sacred for tourists who have been caught chipping pieces off the edges.

After lunch we drove to Bûlak, an interesting suburb of Cairo. The houses are very old, and the street-scenes very curious and thoroughly Eastern in character. The large overhanging windows and casements familiar in pictures are everywhere to be seen, and now and then a glimpse of a female face is caught peeping furtively out at the passers-by. The streets are very narrow, and the coachman yells and shouts at the foot-passengers in his way, not scrupling to apply the whip to quicken their movements. All this is taken patiently—far too much so—and betrays the saddest side of Egyptian character, speaking volumes for the way in which the people have been treated.

Hard by was a curious sight. Standing against a wall, and raised above the level of the street like another Simon Stylites, was a strange-looking man, whose only raiment consisted of a sack, through a hole in which one arm was thrust. In his hand he held a small instrument like a garden-rake, with which he tortured his back, while his gaze " seemed upon the

A Holy Fakir.

future bent." Some irreverent tourists looking on were presently moved to laughter at the peculiar exhibition, upon which the holy man gave them one glance of wonder and pity, and then resumed his gaze into futurity.

It being fair-day, there were a large number of booths, cheap theatres, peep-shows, merry-go-rounds, etc., just as one sees in England. In another place was a story-teller, surrounded by an appreciative audience, who treated every "point" with loud laughter. It was curious to see how earnest and interested they all were, and the dramatic manner in which the story was told.

The National Museum for Egyptian antiquities, founded by Mariette Bey, is situated in Bûlak. Our time being short, we proposed paying it another visit, which, however, we were unfortunately unable to do. Much of the sculpture is really marvellous in its life-like character. One of the most remarkable statues is of wood, and is said to be 4,000 years old. It is admirably carved. There is also a large collection of jewellery, beads, enamels, etc.; chess and draught-boards, an artist's paint-box and brushes, bread, eggs, fruit, pieces of well-made rope and thread; an axe of gilt bronze, having a gilt cedar-wood handle; a gold boat with twelve silver oarsmen, and many other curiosities. The museum is one of the most interesting sights in Egypt, and will well repay many visits.

In the evening some of our party took donkeys and a guide and returned to Bûlak to see some of the shows, but the first they visited was of so extraordinary a character they decided to see no more until their taste was educated up or down to the present Egyptian standard.

IRRIGATION.

The railway journey from Cairo to Alexandria occupied about 6½ hours. The line crosses the Delta of the Nile, the country being very flat all the way.

The soil here is extremely fertile, and it was very interesting to watch the various agricultural operations as we rode along. We particularly noticed the many modes in which water is supplied to the land. Alongside the railway runs a stream issuing from the Nile, and the different holdings of land are bordered with little streamlets in place of hedges.

A WRECKED SHIP OF THE DESERT.

At the junction of these streamlets with the main stream may frequently be seen a couple of men standing on either bank lifting water from the river to the streamlets by means of a huge flat bowl, holding probably eight to ten gallons. This vessel is lifted on either side by means of two long handles diverging from each other, and it is surprising how large a quantity of water can be thrown up by means of it in an hour. The bowl is always in motion with a fine swing, and it is evident the men are working on their own account.

Every station at which we stopped is crowded with people selling oranges, water, etc., and very clever they are at their business too, very persuasive, and as quick as thought to see if you are inclined to buy. The children are the merriest, liveliest things imaginable, with bright eyes and shining white teeth. Here also may be seen numbers of beggars, young and old, calling out eternal *backsheesh*. We saw some venerable old fellows, bent nearly double with age, and with hair and whiskers quite white, who entreated us piteously to help them, saying " Got no mother, got no father, *backsheesh!*" Such orphans as these never obtained our sympathy, although they afforded us great amusement.

While in Cairo, news came of the dissolution of Parliament by Lord Beaconsfield, and we hastened to Alexandria to take the steamer for Italy on the following day; but on arriving we found the weather so excessively rough that the steamers were detained: and, as there seemed no prospect of getting off, we determined to proceed to Port Saïd, by way of Ismaïlia, in order to take the steamer sailing thence for Naples, hoping on some future occasion to be able to see what is to be seen in Alexandria. A day's railway-ride brought us to Ismaïlia, from which place we took the evening mail-boat to Port Saïd. The night was very cold, and after a seven hours' trip on the Canal it was very pleasant to find ourselves in the magnificent hotel built by Prince Henry of the Netherlands, attached to the Dutch factory at Port Saïd.

One of the Orient Steamers was due to sail on the following day, and we expected to proceed to Naples in her, but after providing us with tickets the agent sent us word that she had been detained a week and that we must choose another vessel. There was no other way of escape than by taking the P. and O. Steamer "Mongolia" to Malta, trusting to being able to find a ready means of crossing to Naples from that place. Unfortunately a heavy storm in the Mediterranean had the effect of delaying our arrival in Malta some hours, and we had the mortification of seeing the Naples steamer leaving the harbour as we were entering it. We arrived on Monday and found there would not be another steamer until Thursday, and as the Birmingham election was to take place on Wednesday in the following week our chance of getting there seemed very doubtful. Leaving Malta, however, on the Thursday, by dint of almost continual travelling night and day, we arrived safely in Birmingham at half-past ten on the Wednesday morning, and proceeded at once to register our votes for Bright and Chamberlain, two of the three successful Liberal candidates.

AU REVOIR.

IN THE SUEZ CANAL.

CHAPTER XII.*

AFTER a stormy passage through the Mediterranean we turned in towards Port Saïd, and soon after sighting the handsome lighthouse took the French pilot on board, anchoring broadside on to the main street of the town and within fifty yards of the shore. A motley throng, in boats quite as motley, soon filled up the space between the ship and the shore, and a wild jabber composed of a mixture of English, French, Italian, and Arabic filled the air. Presently the usual tribe of pedlars came on deck, and having spread out their wares invited the passengers to buy, somewhat after the fashion of London tradesmen in Cheapside hundreds of years ago with their cry of "What lack ye?" The inevitable Maltese with his lace, the Greek money-changer walking about with his hands full of silver offering to change, and astonishing the honest Britisher

---

* In a former chapter I gave an account of a voyage to Australia by way of the Cape of Good Hope. On a subsequent visit to the Colonies I went by the Canal route, returning through Egypt overland.

on his first voyage by his liberality in proffering twenty shillings for a sovereign—the rate of exchange, however, leaving him a very good profit. Near him is a Hebrew, whom I remember having seen at Aden, the black curls over his brow reminding one forcibly of Benjamin Disraeli. This man keeps to his trade of dealer in ostrich feathers. Here also are gentlemen of the long robe—not lawyers, but Arabs, in ample white night-shirts and turbans—offering to young ladies in the most seductive tones, at two shillings each, coral necklaces, which can

A FEATHER MERCHANT.

be purchased in Birmingham at three shillings the dozen, while dealers in photographs, melons, and oranges walk about always ready to take one-fourth of what they ask for their wares. Parallel with us are the quays, on which are crowds of people of all nationalities. The Custom House in front is occupied by a company of English artillerymen, the entrance being guarded by a British sentry, while overhead the Egyptian flag is flying. Away to the left is the old Dutch hotel, recently bought by the British Government, and now occupied by two hundred men of the Royal Marine Light Infantry.

Immediately in front of the ship is the main street of the town. It is perfectly straight and about half a mile long, with a small public garden near the end. In this street are a large number of *casinos*, where music is dealt out at nights by bands of female performers, who are called "Bohemiennes," and where, we are assured, everything is properly respectable—until eleven o'clock! Many of our lady passengers, in the innocence of their hearts, looking forward to a pleasant concert during the evening, are much shocked when they learn that the said concerts are held in *casinos*.

We landed at ten o'clock, and had a leisurely walk through the town and halfway through the Arab quarter, but the smells were so offensive that we turned back. A lot of young Arabs, however, urged us to go on farther, for there was an Arab hanging, but as we did not think a dead Arab would be likely to be a more agreeable sight than a living one we declined. The culprit had been executed that morning for the murder of his grand-daughter, nine months previously An account of his crime was written in Arabic and attached to his breast, and the large scissors with which he committed the murder were suspended around his neck. Some of the young Arabs were vexed with us because we would not give them *backsheesh*, and began to be insulting, talking about Arabi, when presently a smart youth of ten years old interfered, and, cuffing the ears of the young monkeys, loudly proclaimed the prowess of the British.

We went to look at the Dutch House where the Marines were quartered, and a young officer, Lieutenant Cotter, kindly asked us to go over the building. The rooms are very fine; but what a change in the scene since we slept here for a night two-and-a-half years ago! Then the hotel was in operation, and the rooms were furnished as elaborately as in the house of an English gentleman. But everything had been taken away, and the officers were sleeping on the marble floors, and the men on the floors of the adjoining warehouses, where also the horses were stabled. Lieutenant Cotter had made a bedstead for himself, and one of his men had made him a bath, and these, with a chair, completed the furnishing of his room; his wash-basin consisted of a large flower-pot, with a cork in the hole at the bottom. The Marines arrived in Egypt a few days after Tel-el-Kebir, and so saw no fighting; but they had to march over to Fort Gemileh, seven miles away, and fully expected a very severe fight, as the fort is heavily armed with modern guns, and was manned by Nubians, who are reported to be excellent soldiers. Fortunately, however, there was no need to fight, as the commander recognised that the war was over.

At night a number of our passengers, of all classes, went ashore to attend the concert, and one of them known as Cetewayo, *alias* the Carrib or the Pirate King, announced his intention of kicking up a great row at the *casino* (of course *after* eleven o'clock), and he was as good as his word, and others besides, several having to be locked up for the night. We visited the soldiers in the barracks, and they were very glad to have a chat. We sent them the newspapers we had brought from England, with which they were greatly pleased. They told us the numbers, variety, and voracity of the insects was something maddening; some being busy at night, and others during the day, and that it was almost impossible to keep oneself decent. Altogether Port Saïd must be a dreadful place for Englishmen to live in; there was very little society, and I was told that at the time there was only one unmarried lady left.

The commanding officer of the Marines told us that the principal duty they had to perform as "police" was to keep the English sailors and visitors in order, almost all the drunkenness and trouble coming from them—to our disgrace be it said.

The land all along the coast lies very low, and is not seen until the yellowish-green water near it is reached. The water is discoloured by the mud of the Nile, one of the mouths of which (the Tanitic) is situated a little to the west of Port Saïd. This ceaseless flow of mud was one of the greatest difficulties experienced in making the Canal, and necessitated important and expensive works to prevent its access to the harbour. Lake Menzaleh is formed by this Nile mouth, and covers an area of about 1,000 square miles. Good wildfowl shooting is to be had there, and there are numbers of flamingoes and other birds. Port Saïd, as is well known, owes its origin to the Canal, and is situated on an island separating Lake Menzaleh from the Mediterranean. The town was expected by M. de Lesseps to progress very rapidly—indeed to rival Alexandria, but it has not gone ahead so fast as he expected. At present there are about 12,000 people there, and I should say more than half are Europeans. The town is built very regularly, and consists of rather temporary brick and wooden houses. The making of the harbour was a very difficult work. It occupies 570 acres, and is excavated to a depth of 26ft. Two massive piers protect it, running out to the sea in a north-easterly direction for about a mile and a half. At starting they are 1,440 yards apart, narrowing to 770 yards, the navigable entrance being about 150 yards wide. The piers are constructed of artificial stone, composed of seven parts of sand from the desert, and of one part of hydraulic lime from France. The concrete was mixed by machinery, and then poured into great wooden moulds, where it remained for weeks, after which the wood was taken away to allow of the blocks hardening. Each block weighed twenty tons, and contained $18\frac{1}{2}$ cubic yards; no fewer than 25,000 of these blocks were used in constructing the breakwater. The lighthouse is a very handsome structure, and is also formed of blocks of concrete; it is 164ft. high, and can be seen twenty-four miles away, being fitted with the electric light. *(Baedeker.)*

At 4.30 p.m. our vessel started for the Canal, and having safely entered it made fast for the night, as no travelling is allowed after sunset. During the evening myriads of gnats and mosquitoes came on to the ship, the electric light being absolutely dimmed by them in many places, and we had good reason to expect a trying night from their presence.

While our ship's doctor and a party of friends were ashore at Port Saïd they were greatly amused by the attention of a number of Arab lads who followed them everywhere. During their walk in the native quarter the party came upon a great crowd, and one of the young Arabs referring to the man who had been hanged during the morning stated that the man was not an Arab, but a Greek, and proceeded to explain the distinguishing characteristics of the various nationalities represented at this cosmopolitan port; he said—

"The Greek, he bery bat man, he stab—so (with a vigorous motion as though stabbing an opponent in the chest).

" 'gyptian, he bery goot man, he only slap, so.

" English man, he bery goot man (striking an attitude); he say ' Come on and box.'

" English man—he bery goot man.

" English man—he bery goot man.

" Melikan man—he bery goot man.

" Melikan man—he bery goot man.

" 'talian man—he bery bat man."

Ending with a very uncomplimentary allusion to our Irish fellow-subjects.

What is wanted to make Port Saïd really prosperous is a railway from the interior to bring the produce from the cotton and wheat fields, and then the steamers which bring the coals could at once load up for home, saving the necessity of going empty to Alexandria for their homeward freights. Last year 540,000 tons of coal were sold at Port Saïd, and all the ships which brought it had to go away empty. But so long as the Canal Company are entitled to all the Customs dues at Port Saïd, it is not to be expected that the Egyptian Government will favour the construction of such a line.

Some of our fellow-passengers were members of the Blue Ribbon Army, and although they were by no means obtrusive in supporting their views, being contented for the most part with wearing the "bit of blue"— others resented this reasonable liberty, styling it an impertinence, and formed themselves into an opposition Order, which they called the *Red* Ribbon Army, and they busied themselves in enlisting recruits. It was noticeable that, with the exception of an old *roué* or two, only young men with small heads and long legs, who, if they ever indulged in reading, confined their choice to books translated or adapted from the French, composed the rank and file, the officers being older men, who were not often seen out of the gambling or smoke-room. One of these latter was called the "Spider," because from an early hour in the morning he sat in the smoke-room waiting to "play" with any who might choose to try conclusions with him.

The Patron and President of the Society was a noble lord, and certainly a better choice could not have been made. Amongst the rules of the Society were these:—

> Any member found without his red ribbon is to be fined in drinks all round.
> Members are to be neither too drunk nor too sober.
> Members must never go to bed quite sober.
> Members must never refuse a drink.

The President certainly set a fair example in his endeavour to perform the duties of his office, and would never be mistaken for a member of the *Blue* Ribbon Army, even if he did not wear the badge, for good wine had marked him for its own. Under the fostering influence of such rules and such a "noble" example, it is not to be wondered at that the Army showed a blatant front to the enemy, and that their proceedings soon became disorderly. At this juncture some good-natured moderate men joined the Reds, with the view, it appears, of moderating their offensive tactics, and the result was a manifesto which set forth, amongst other things—That the Red Ribbon Army entertained no feelings of ill-will toward those who did not agree with them, and invited all to join their ranks, and that they assured abstainers that there was always iced water on the sideboard of the smoke room for their convenience. One of the chiefs of the Reds was a dark man, already referred to as Cetewayo, *alias* the Carrib. I one day heard this worthy call one of the Reds to account for appearing without his badge, the defaulting member replying that he had "resigned." "That won't do," said the Carrib, "Once a member always a member; come and pay up." Yes, I thought, when the devil has once got his claws in a man retreat is all but impossible.

Every one of the young fellows who joined the Reds fell into the "Spider's" web, and were most of them eased of their spare cash through the agency of a pack of cards.

This "Spider" was one day on deck sitting by the side of one of my friends who had just awaked from a doze, to whom he said, "You have had a nap?" "Yes," I said, "Mr. —— takes his nap on deck in the face of day, but you have yours in the dimness of the smoke-room" (alluding to the game of "Nap"). "That's true," said he, "I like to play when the light is somewhat dull. These fellows say I am always winning. Well, suppose I am? They keep coming to me, and in Melbourne if they consult an expert on any subject they have to pay two guineas, and I take no less." "You take no less, and don't refuse more," said I. "Exactly, that is just it," said the Spider, and he was said to have cleared out most of the card-playing fraternity. Ultimately, the almost unvaried success of the Spider caused a general feeling to be raised against him amongst the gamblers; but as long as there still remained some who had not been relieved of their money, and others whom the Spider had allowed to win from him occasionally, this feeling did not exist to any great extent. One evening, however, the Pirate charged the web-spinner with having cheated him, and a general disturbance ensued, the Pirate assuring the Spider that as soon as they quitted the ship he would soundly thrash him with a whip, which he displayed, so we were in hopes of having a little excitement on leaving the vessel. One result, however, was to practically dissolve the Red Ribbon army, and the Carrib then came out in a new character. At the fancy dress ball held on the promenade deck he appeared in a dress suit, and was at once saluted with the cry, "Here's a lark, Cetewayo disguised as a *gentleman!*"

The noble President of the Reds was somewhat of a curiosity in his way, a very kind-hearted sympathetic man, as many a poor invalid in the second and third classes could testify. The doctor told us of many instances of his lordship's kindness in visiting some of the sick third-class passengers, and giving them dainties from his private stores; and I heard one poor woman tell him she should never forget him for his goodness to her husband. Some of our colonial passengers, wishing to make the most of their unusual proximity to nobility, were too persevering in their

CETEWAYO DISGUISED AS A GENTLEMAN.

attentions to his lordship, and evidently bored him; but the tact with which he "shunted" them, and the studied politeness of his language, did not prevent onlookers detecting a silent "confound their impudence" terminating each reply. Once, in referring to the pertinacity of these people, he remarked to a bystander, in a hissing tone, "One *must* be civ-il." The noble lord took a great interest in everything pertaining to sailors; his regard for them was evidently warm and genuine. While we were passing through the Canal, coming to our anchorage for the night, we found the space at our disposal was very limited, as the vessels were numerous, consequently our men had to be very active in getting the ship into her berth. I was standing by his lordship's side, looking at the sailors running along the sandbank, carrying the heavy cable as nimbly as though it was a fishing line. Lord —— was delighted, and, turning to me, and in his funny fashion grasping his clothes in front of the place where his stomach should be, exclaimed in tones of rapture, "Look at our *de-ah* blue-jackets, look!"

His lordship was very popular with the young men on board, but I hope he did not often make such observations to them, as one young gentleman informed me he had made to him, speaking of his past life. "I have committed many sins in my time," said his lordship, "and I hope to live to commit many more."

CHAPTER XIII.

RETURNING from Australia we touched at Colombo, where my companion and a friend paid an interesting visit to Arabi, who invited them to dine with him. It soon became evident that intercourse would have to be conducted through interpreters, as Arabi understood neither French nor English, and his visitors were ignorant of Arabic.

My friend was an invalid, and the first dish put on the table caused him great anxiety, as it was one which his medical man had given him strict orders to avoid. What was to be done? My companion explained to the invalid that in the East no greater affront could be given to a host than to decline to partake of what was offered, and so, not having provided himself with Jack the Giant Killer's device for disposing of surplus food, he was fain to eat it, not without certain fearful forebodings.

Arabi's personal appearance had greatly altered, he having grown a beard which was turning grey. At the table with him were his two sons, lads apparently of ten and twelve years respectively. On his left sat Fehmi Pasha, a man of very striking appearance with a face indicating considerable intellectual power. Arabi desired to know what the English thought of him, a question which my companion parried by saying the English always respected a brave man. Rising to take leave of the host, my companion patted the head of the eldest boy in a kindly manner. This seemed to move Arabi in a singular way. He rose and said, in a sharp tone of command, to his boys, "Salaam," then, crossing the room and placing his hand on my companion's shoulder, said with some emotion, " Ah, ah, good, good."

Proceeding on our voyage we called at Aden, a dreadful place, without a single redeeming feature, in European eyes. Those of our countrymen who are compelled to reside here in the service of the country are entitled to the deepest sympathy of every Englishman. The possession of Aden is of considerable importance to England and to India, both as a coaling station and as a military post, although in the latter respect it is of less importance than formerly. The islands commanding the channels at the entrance to the Red Sea are after all the key to the position, one of the most important being the Island of Perim, the acquisition of which does more credit to the '*cuteness* of the British commander at Aden than to his sense of honour—that is, if the story told of him be true. It is related that one evening, nearly forty years ago, two

French war-ships cast anchor before Aden, and the English governor with a laudable desire to ascertain the object of their visit invited the commanders of the ships to dinner. Unfortunately for France the officers were not teetotallers, and the weather being hot and the British commander's wine strong, the gallant Frenchmen's tongues were loosened, and the perfidious Englishman ascertained that the mission with which his guests were charged was no less than the occupa-

ADENESE WOMEN.

tion of the Island of Perim in the name of Louis Philippe, King of the French! Without losing a moment the governor sent orders to the captain of the English gunboat lying at Aden to proceed with all speed and in the strictest secresy to take possession of the island in the name of the Queen! The sun had risen before the festivities at the governor's residence had ceased, and then with many bows his guests departed to their ships, and shortly afterwards left

Aden for their destination. On arrival, their astonishment and mortification may be imagined when they saw on the highest point on the island the British flag flying, and the gunboat which they had seen at Aden on the previous day anchored close inshore. The incident gave occasion for much tall talk at the time on the part of the fiery French colonels, and, not without reason, I fear, gave fresh life to the cry of "Perfidious Albion."

We arrived at Suez in the third week of February, and as soon as our steamer stopped, our old dragoman Hassan came on board with a huge packet of letters for us, and although he had only seen us once before, three years ago, he not only remembered our names but came straight to us and told us he had brought a boat for our use, and that bedrooms were engaged for us at the hotel. We owed all this attention—which was most seasonable, as I was still suffering from the effects of a malarious fever contracted in Australia—to Messrs. Cook and Son, who had been advised of my coming, and here I will say that in Egypt and Syria the name of "Cook" is the talisman which solves all difficulties and robs travelling of nearly all its inconveniences.

On landing we were forcibly struck with the altered demeanour of the people since our previous visit. On that occasion landing was effected under the greatest difficulties. The people seemed to look upon us as fair prey. It was almost impossible for us to keep our luggage together, and the insolent threatening manner in which *backsheesh* was demanded was not a little disturbing to those who were visiting an Eastern country for the first time. But now all was changed; instead of idle excited crowds loitering everywhere, everyone seemed to be engaged in some work, *backsheesh* was rarely asked for, and always in subdued tones, and one refusal was enough. Even the donkey boys had been reached, for when their proffered services were declined they went away with a "thank you."

The Suez Hotel is kept by an Englishman, and he informed us that during the war he left it in charge of natives, and found everything safe and in order on his return.

On the following day we proceeded by railway to Cairo, *viâ* Ismaïlia and Tel-el-Kebir. At many of the stations British soldiers were on guard, a part of their duty appearing to be the inspection of the natives' baggage; this was done amidst much good humour on both sides—indeed, all through Egypt the British soldier seemed to be on the best possible terms with the people, as indeed there is every reason why he should be, for it is certain he has been the means of saving the people of Egypt from a tyranny of the worst kind—the tyranny of rapacious pachas, civil and military. With the usual exclusiveness of our nation, our party of four had arranged to have the whole of the compartment of the railway-carriage to ourselves. It is true we paid extra for the convenience, but at one of the stations, the train being very crowded, two Frenchmen endeavoured to enter, being prevented, however, by the Arab conductor. The Frenchmen, with much gesticulation and great volubility, pointed out to the Arab that there were only four persons in the carriage, whereas it was constructed to take eight; the guard insisted that there *were* eight persons in the compartment, although it was patent to all that there were only four. "Four!" said the Frenchmen. "Eight!" returned the guard, giving us a most wicked wink, which, however, failed to extort *backsheesh*. Ultimately our would-be companions were safely bestowed elsewhere.

The railway passes by the field of Tel-el-Kebir, the entrenchments stretching as far as the eye can reach. When my companion went over the ground a few weeks after the battle it was covered with débris of every kind, clothing, arms, ammunition, and other ghastly indications of a battle-field.

In one of the entrenchments my friend found a leaf torn from the New Testament, while only a yard or two away was a leaf from the Koran, and hard by he picked up a letter written in Arabic, addressed to a soldier on the field, requesting him to authorise the writer to collect his rents in Cairo.

On reaching the station of Tel-el-Kebir we found a number of tourists who had come up from Cairo to gather curiosities from the battle-field, but since my friend's visit in the autumn everything had been cleared off, and the new comers were gathering pebbles (!) as mementoes of the famous engagement.

The little grave-yard in which the British troops are buried is situated near to the station, and appeared to be kept in excellent order.

In Cairo, as in Suez, the absence of the feverish excitement, latent insolence, and spirit of unrest, so apparent during our last visit, was very noticeable. There, too, *backsheesh* was rarely demanded, and most of the people seemed to have something to do.

It was curious to see the English soldiers lounging about the town in all directions. They seemed to be quite at home. One of them informed me he had gone through the Transvaal campaign, but very much preferred the land of Goshen!

While we were in Cairo we often expressed our wonder that the city was ever free from cholera or some other deadly epidemic. The sanitary condition of the streets and public places was shocking in the extreme.

Fronting the Opera House and the great hotels and Government offices are the extensive Ezbekîyeh public gardens, enclosed with iron railings. Around the outside is a very handsome paved footpath, which, although in the very heart of the city, is in many places, utterly impassable because of the unspeakable horrors accumulated upon it. If the English occupation of Egypt does nothing more than cause the towns of that country to be properly cleansed, it will be the means of saving as many lives every few years as were lost in the late campaign.

There are two classes of people who undoubtedly view the British occupation of Egypt with great and well-founded dislike—the military party and the pachas. These classes have always played into each other's hands, and always at the expense of the down-trodden and patient fellaheen—the backbone and mainstay of the country. For the latter class the presence of the British army is an almost unmixed blessing.

From time immemorial the desirability of connecting the Mediterranean and Red Seas by a canal has been fully recognised; but the work does not appear to have been attempted before the reign of Pharaoh Necho, who undertook to construct a canal between the Nile and the Red Sea. In carrying out this work 120,000 Egyptians perished, and before it was completed the King abandoned it, having been informed by the Oracle that the foreigners alone would profit by the work. Eventually the canal was completed under the rule of Darius the Persian, and of the Ptolemies.

The canal was carried through the lakes Balah and Menzaleh, another branch being constructed to the Bitter Lakes, into which the fresh water canal—watering the land of Goshen—emptied itself; but owing to the constant state of war it fell into decay, and was abandoned.

Many suggestions as to the reopening of the waterway have been made in almost every generation since. Bonaparte, during his expedition to Egypt in 1798, even caused the preliminary works to be undertaken. His chief engineer surveyed the ground, but, owing to a serious miscalculation, threw great doubt on the possibility of carrying out the work. He estimated the level of the Red Sea to be nearly 33ft. higher than that of the Mediterranean, an idea that Leibnitz ridiculed nearly a century before. Vigorous protests against Lepère's theory were not wanting, but it was, nevertheless, sufficient to cause the abandonment of the scheme until Monsieur Lesseps directed his attention to the matter. On his appointment as an Attaché to the French Mission, Lesseps had to undergo a lengthy quarantine at Alexandria; here he was supplied with books by his Consul, among them being Lepère's memoirs respecting the scheme for connecting the two seas, the effect of which upon the young Frenchman's mind was never effaced.

In 1847 a Commission of Engineers demonstrated the inaccuracy of Lepère's observations, and proved that the level of the two seas was practically the same. In 1854 Lesseps having matured his plan laid it before the Viceroy, who determined to carry it out. Palmerston, then premier, did his utmost, from political motives, to thwart the enterprise; but early in 1856 permission was given to commence the work.

Considerable difficulty was experienced in raising the capital, but on the 25th April, 1858, operations were actually begun. The Viceroy undertook to pay many of the current expenses, and provided 25,000 workmen, who were to be paid and fed by the Company at an inexpensive rate, and were to be relieved every three months. In order to provide these men with water 4,000 casks suitable for being carried on camels had to be made, and 1,600 of these animals were daily employed in bringing supplies, at a cost of £320 per day.

At the end of December, 1863, the Fresh Water Canal was completed, by which the Company was relieved of the enormous expense of supplying the workmen with water.

On the 18th March, 1869, the water of the Mediterranean was allowed to flow into the nearly dry salt-incrusted basins of the Bitter Lakes, some parts of which lay forty feet below the level of the Mediterranean, while others required extensive dredging operations. The Bitter Lakes have been identified with the Marah of the Bible (Exodus xv., 23—" And when they came to Marah, they could not drink of the waters of Marah for they were bitter"). The captain of our vessel informed me that in these lakes the saltness, and consequently the density of the water, is such as to cause the vessel to rise five inches above the ordinary water-line.

The cost of constructing the Canal amounted to about £19,000,000, more than a third of which was contributed by the Khedive. The original capital of the company in 400,000 shares amounted to £8,000,000, the difference being raised by loans payable at fixed intervals, and adding an annual burden to the scheme of £451,000. The festivities connected with the opening of the Canal in 1869 cost the Khedive—that is to say the taxpayer of Egypt—£4,200,000, or more than half the total capital!

The great mercantile importance of the Canal is apparent from the following data:—Between London and Bombay forty-four per cent. of the distance is saved by through-going ships; between London and Hong Kong twenty-eight per cent., and between Marseilles and Bombay fifty-nine per cent. Over eighty per cent. of the trade passing through the Canal is done in British vessels, and in 1875—or six years after the Canal was opened—the English traffic was equal to twelve times that of the French.

In 1870, 486 steamers, representing 493,911 tons, passed through the canal, and in 1882 these figures had risen to 3,198 steamers with 7,125,000 tons. *(Baedeker.)*

From Port Saïd the Canal runs in a nearly straight line to Kantara (a mere group of sheds), its course lying across the shallow lagoon-like Lake Menzaleh, which has an average depth of only three feet. The embankments are low, irregular sand-banks, formed of the dredged material, and having at the margin of the water a coarse growth of straggling sedgy-looking vegetation. After passing Kantara, the Balah Lakes are reached, and the course is marked out in their open surface by a double line of buoys. Then the most difficult portion of the original work is reached—viz., the cutting of El Guisr, which is six miles long, the depth from ground-level to surface of water being about forty-five feet. This is by far the highest land in the Isthmus. Leaving the El Guisr cutting, the open waters of Lake Timsah *(Crocodile Lake)* are reached, and far away across its blue mirror-like surface stretches the double line of buoys, marking out the track. On the northern shore of the lake, buried in a delightful mass of vegetation, lies the French town of Ismaïlia, once the great centre from which operations during the construction of the Canal were conducted, and now one of the principal stations whence its navigation is controlled by means of telegraph. Lake Timsah has an area of some six or seven square miles, and the huge fleet of war vessels, transports, and tenders which Lord Wolseley used as a base for his operations in the late campaign lay there without difficulty. From Lake Timsah the Suez Canal holds a roughly parallel course with the Freshwater Canal and the Suez line of railway, and passes through a long cutting into the Bitter Lakes, an extremely tame and uninteresting sheet of water some fifteen miles long, with flat, low, sandy banks, and thence into another long cutting— some twenty-six feet deep at Shalouf—after which the flat sandy plains of Suez are traversed, and the head of the gulf reached.

The impression is general that the Suez Canal is cut through immense deposits of sand, or sand and water, but this is quite erroneous. The desert, it is true, is sandy and sterile, but the sand is quite superficial, covering a gypseous clay, not at all difficult to work in. From Balah to the Bitter Lakes there is fine muddy sand, with clay at intervals, and at Serapeum a rocky barrier. From the Bitter Lakes to Suez, however, there is a good clay, with limestone at Shalouf. The sinuosities in the Canal are such as to render the passage of vessels over 400 feet long somewhat difficult. It was expected that these curves would prevent the washing away of the banks, but it is doubtful whether they have at all contributed to the preservation of the sandy embankments. Indeed, most of the predictions of the early destruction of the Canal by the operation of natural causes have been proved to be as ill-founded as such predictions generally are. The banks have no ill-regulated propensity for crumbling away. The Canal is *not* in perpetual and imminent danger of being silted-up. The enormous and costly dredging operations that were to swallow more than the revenue of the undertaking are unknown, and the sole matter for regret is that the Canal was not made as wide again as it is, for the accommodation of the vast traffic it has created. Among the many confident prophesies made by professional engineers of the day, one stands recorded in the technical papers to the effect that every vessel must necessarily be towed through the Canal, the explanation being that the regulation speed of five miles per hour was not sufficient to afford steering "way"; hence, said the prophet, the slightest wind across the line of the Canal must infallibly blow ashore any vessel whose commander should have the temerity to attempt to steam between the two seas. Experience, however, has shown that the largest vessels are under perfect command when propelled by their own engines.

It is impossible for anyone to pass through the Canal without being impressed with the urgent necessity for vastly increased accommodation for the constantly augmenting traffic. The delays occasioned by the difficulties in coaling, the blocks in the Canal—caused sometimes by the enormous traffic, and sometimes by the sinking of a ship across the narrow channel—are most vexatious. No less than five days elapsed between the time of the arrival of our steamer at Port Saïd and of its departure from Suez, a distance of less than one hundred miles.

In every way it is most unfortunate for English commerce that—thanks to the mulish obstinacy of Lord Palmerston—the management of the Canal should have been thrown into the hands of Frenchmen; for, while according the highest meed of praise to M. de Lesseps for his genius, tenacity of purpose, and energy, in designing and carrying out such a vast undertaking in the teeth of obstacles which would have daunted most men, it is impossible to ignore the fact that, as compared with English traffic-managers, the French officials responsible for the working of the Canal are vastly inferior in capacity. The spirit of officialism as displayed by a liberal use of red tape, and a certain non-elasticity in carrying out the laws, so familiar to all travellers in France, exists in an intensified form in the local management of the Canal. To the ordinary traveller through the Canal, for example, it seems absurd that vessels should be stopped for the night while some hours of light remain, yet as soon as the sun goes down no further advance can be made. Again, although daylight comes long before sunrise, it is forbidden to move till the sun is up. Then again, experience shows that by the use of the electric light the largest vessels can be handled with the utmost ease. An electric light fixed in the foremast of a ship sweeps the Canal from bank to bank, and for all practical purposes gives a light equal to that of day; it seems strange, therefore, that vessels possessing such appliances should not be permitted to proceed during the night. If one ventures to make such a suggestion to a Canal official, he at once replies that the rules laid down for the regulation of the traffic forbid night passages, and if one further ventures to remind him that the said rules were made before the introduction of electric lighting, he shrugs his shoulders and plainly intimates that you have tried his patience long enough.

A little delegation of authority from the chief office to the pilot or other Canal official on board the ships would at once result in a vast diminution of delay, and consequently in an increase to the capability of the Canal, but the genius of French administration appears to be opposed to the granting of any latitude or freedom of action to inferior officials, and so in the administration of the Canal everything is done by the official at the chief office in Ismaïlia, who transmits his orders by telegraph.

But, after all the practicable improvements in the navigation of the present Canal have been made, the necessity for a new one will be no less urgent, and it is especially unfortunate that the Conservative party should have made negotiations with M. de Lesseps so difficult by openly suggesting that we should use our accidental supremacy in Egypt to advance the national interests, without regard to the rights possessed by him. Whatever the actual status of M. de Lesseps, under his concession, may be, it is clear that he has always considered he had a monopoly. At the outset he endeavoured to enlist British sympathy and capital in his undertaking by demonstrating that the bulk of the traffic must necessarily come from English sources. Was it probable, therefore, he would have spent the Company's capital in making the Canal if, after having demonstrated its success, an English company were at liberty to make another, alongside, and take away four-fifths of its traffic?

In business matters the French are proverbially short-sighted. They fail to see that "three sixpences are better than one shilling," and are consequently unwilling to surrender present advantages without an absolute certainty of an early and great benefit arising from their doing so. They are much more truly a nation of retailers or shopkeepers than the English are, notwithstanding Napoleon's famous epithet. What is wanted is a greater breadth of view in the administration of the Canal, and it is in this respect that it is particularly unfortunate there is not a larger English representation on the Board of Management. If we had a representation equal to our share of the capital, the result would soon be apparent in the adoption of a line of policy giving the utmost facilities to the Canal's customers, to the great advantage of both.

The recent discussions upon the Suez Canal question cannot fail to be of the greatest use to the Government when they reopen negotiations with M. de Lesseps, and if the latter finds it impossible to make another canal without a further concession of land, he may probably think it advisable to conciliate his partner and chief customer by making greater concessions in return for the influence of the British Government with that of the Khedive and the Sultan on his behalf.

But even if no further advantages for British commerce be obtained from the Canal Company, this country occupies a unique position as regards communication with the East. In less than fifteen years the whole of the original cost of the British shares, both principal and interest, will have been paid out of profits, and the Chancellor of the Exchequer of the day will have to decide as to the destination of the revenue which the shares produce. It appears to me that, after making provision for the necessary expenses attending the administration of the property, it would be both just and politic to return the balance to the owners of the ships whose use of the Canal has been the means of creating the revenue. If this course be adopted British commerce will be immensely benefited, for our ships will be able to use the Canal at a little more than half the expense falling upon those of other nations, and this great advantage will have been obtained without having cost the British taxpayer a single penny. The money will simply be returned into the hands which contributed it, and the proposal, therefore, does not in any way partake of the character of a bounty.

What is known as the Dual Control was established in 1879. By it the British and French Controllers-General were invested with considerable powers over the administration of the finances, in addition to which the Khedive undertook to assign a certain portion of the revenue for the discharge of the national obligations.

In the following year a Law of Liquidation, as drawn up by the Commissioners appointed for the purpose, was issued with the agreement of all the interested European Powers.

In return for these concessions, the Foreign Bondholders made a compromise with the Egyptian Government involving the surrender of a considerable portion of their claims. This settlement, while relieving the country from an enormous burden, placed it in a position to meet its liabilities and to progress in the development of its resources, and, in the language of Lord Granville in his despatch to Lord Dufferin, "it was undoubtedly working well for the material prosperity of the country, and promised to do so for the future;" and in a subsequent despatch the Foreign Secretary declared that, through the action of the Control, great advantages had been secured for the natives, such as "the spread of education, the abolition of vexatious taxation, the establishment of the land-tax on a regular and equitable basis, and the diminution of forced labour."

Our dragoman, an intelligent Copt, fully corroborated Lord Granville's statement. He said that all that the Egyptian people required was moderate taxation, certainty as to its amount and as to the time of its collection, and such a military law as would relieve them from the press-gang. He further said that before the institution of the Control, whenever the Khedive wanted a new ironclad, or a new palace, or half a dozen additional inmates for his harem, he ordered a new tax to be levied; this tax was sold to some of the rapacious pachas about the Palace, and resold by them to professional tax-gatherers. These wretches committed the greatest atrocities upon the miserable fellaheen, exacting the uttermost farthing under the threat, and often the actual application, of torture; "but now," said my informant, "although the taxes are heavy, their amount is known, and they are collected in coin after the harvest has been gathered."

The country was becoming very prosperous, and there was a surplus in the Treasury when, in February, 1881, a military riot broke out, originating in the arrest of certain Egyptian officers, among whom was the Colonel of the 1st Regiment. The officers of this regiment broke into the Council Room of the Ministry of War, ill-treated the Minister, and then, having released the prisoners, proceeded to the Khedive's Palace, followed by the men of the regiment. In menacing tones they demanded the dismissal of the Minister of War, and redress for their grievances. Arabi Bey was one of the chief actors in this revolt. The Khedive was compelled to submit, the mutinous colonels were reinstated, and tranquillity was restored for the time.

The army officers were not long, however, in showing what their principal object was, for in a few weeks after the revolt, decrees were issued increasing the pay of the army and navy to the extent of nearly £60,000 a year. The Controllers-General had now become aware that everything was at the disposal of the military party, and that the Minister could not guarantee that the officers would not next day insist upon fresh financial concessions. The next demand made by the colonels was that nominations to vacant posts in regiments should rest with them, and this was granted. The object of all this was clear enough—indeed, Arabi declared at one of the meetings of the Commission that "he would not yield unconditional obedience to the War Minister." As time went on fresh symptoms of disaffection broke out, all indicating the determination of the military party to throw off all control and restraint. In September the Ministry was dismissed at the instance of these same men, who throughout the remainder of the year continued a harassing series of turbulent outbreaks, gradually increasing in audacity, and more and more trenching upon matters of administration. They went so far as to demand an increase in the army, involving an annual addition to the estimates of £280,000, although the Controllers declared that not nearly half that amount was available.

The principal figure in all these outbreaks was Arabi, who steadily kept himself at the head of the disaffected party, and gradually increased his influence. After being appointed Under Secretary of War, then Chief Secretary, he was described by Sir E. Malet as having become "Arbiter of the destinies of the country." In March he was made Pasha, and the Khedive was compelled to assent to a number of promotions by Arabi, who insisted on dispensing with the examination required by law for officers. In a word, the real power had become vested in the chiefs of the military party, and the objects of those chiefs were showing themselves more and more evidently to be, increase of the army, increase of pay, and promotion of a large number of officers to high military rank—the desire of all such men in every country of the world.

In the following month Arabi caused numerous arrests to be made among the officers and soldiery in consequence of an alleged conspiracy to murder him. Among the prisoners was the Minister of War, who had been dismissed at the demand of the mutinous regiments in the previous February. The prisoners were tried by a court-martial—irregularly constituted—and the proceedings were kept secret, while no counsel were allowed for the defence. It was generally believed that torture had been used to extort confession. Forty officers were condemned to exile for life to the farthest limits of the Soudan. The Khedive, with great courage, refused to sanction the sentence, and issued a decree commuting it to simple banishment from Egypt.

In the meantime the excitement continued to increase, and the Governments of France and England decided to send a naval force to Alexandria for the protection of the interests of their subjects in Egypt. The combined fleet arrived at Alexandria on the 20th of May. On June 11th the great riot and massacre of Europeans took place, Arabi in the meanwhile erecting new earthworks and strengthening the forts, in spite of his repeated assurances to the contrary. On July 11th, the French fleet having withdrawn, and twenty-four hours' notice having expired, Admiral Seymour opened fire on the forts, and after a few hours completely silenced them; not, however, without his ships having suffered considerably in the encounter.

The above is a sketch of Arabi's career from the time of his first coming into public notice to the time when he became Dictator. He was at no pains to conceal his character as a military adventurer, and every successive step in his career proves him to have been no other. It is true that during the last few weeks he appeared to carry the country with him, which, however, is not difficult to account for, seeing that he was "master of the legions," and that detachments of the army had been sent out into the highways and byways to compel men to come in at the point of the bayonet. In ordinary times it is no uncommon thing to see a chain-gang going through the streets of Egyptian towns composed, not of criminals, but of unhappy wretches brought in by the press-gang for service in the army, and should any of them falter in their steps through weariness or despair, the heavy stick of the driver is always ready to descend upon their shoulders. The only effect of the success of the movement headed by Arabi would have been the perpetuation and extension of this terrible state of things; and yet this is the man who has been persistently held up to the admiration of the world as a pure-minded patriot by a large section of what is called the Peace Party in

England. In the towns Arabi and his agents worked upon the cupidity of the lower orders by telling them that he intended to drive the foreigners into the sea, and that their property should be given over to a general *loot*. In the country districts, where the fellaheen are ground down under the heel of the usurer —always a foreigner, as the Koran forbids usury— Arabi promised to cancel the village debts, and banish the usurers;* while in Upper Egypt, where usury is less common, he appealed to Mohammedan fanaticism. But nowhere did he appeal to a national sentiment,† until, indeed, by various devices, he had become absolute master of the country, when perhaps he thought he might say *L'Etat, c'est moi*.

---

* It is understood that the Khedive's English financial adviser is about to take in hand the case of the Fellaheen *versus* the Usurers. It may aid him to know how a similar state of things in a neighbouring country was dealt with about 2000 years ago.

"Lucullus, Roman general, in his wars against Mithridates, having occupied many cities in Asia which had long been a prey to tax-farmers and usurers, undertook to relieve the people from the extreme misery to which they had been reduced, and set about redeeming the properties given as security to the rapacious money-lenders. He first greatly reduced the rate of interest; secondly, where the interest exceeded the principal he struck it off. He then ordered that the creditor should receive the fourth part of the debtor's income, but if in making his claim any creditor had added the interest to the principal, it was utterly disallowed. By these means, in the space of four years, all debts were paid, and the lands returned to the rightful owners."—*Plutarch's Lives*.

† Report of Mr. Villiers Stuart, M.P., to Lord Dufferin on "The Social and Economical Condition of the People."

CHAPTER XIV.

 WRETCHED journey of over eight hours by rail brought us to Alexandria shortly before midnight. A fierce gale with rain prevailed during most of the journey, and owing to the dilapidated condition of the carriage, waterproofs were necessary to protect us from the rain, which, in spite of closed windows, found access to every part of the compartment. The line itself and the whole of the rolling stock were in a miserable condition of disrepair, and utterly unfit for traffic.

The drive from the railway station to the Hotel Abbat gave us our first glimpse of the ruin wrought by the rioters. The raging storm and drenching sleet were singularly in accord with the scene of desolation and misery on every hand. After the long and cold railway journey, and the drive in the open vehicle from the station, we were in hopes of finding comfortable quarters in the hotel, but the wretchedness prevailing outside seemed to have penetrated into every corner of the establishment. It was impossible to get anything hot to eat, and the cold meats were most uninviting. The proprietor, expecting another train in about an hour, deferred serving even this cold cheer until its arrival. Meanwhile nothing remained for us but to try to warm ourselves by pacing up and down the scantily-furnished

A FAMILIAR FACE.

salle à manger. We were glad to get to bed notwithstanding that the carpts in the beedrooms were flapping in the wind in the most vigorous manner during the night.

On rising next morning we found the storm had not abated, indeed it continued with undiminished fury during the whole of our stay. Our time, however, being limited, it was necessary to disregard the weather in order to visit the scene of the recent operations and the ruins of the city. On leaving the hotel our dragoman of three years ago, Kalifa, at once recognised us, and under his guidance we made a tour of the fortresses, going first to Ras-el-Tin. We found the palace of that name, which forms the landward boundary of the fortress, still partially in ruins and apparently deserted. One could not help feeling that the architect, in selecting such a site for a royal residence, must have regarded the possibility of an attack upon the fort from the sea as being too remote to be taken into account. Some of the other forts had at one time stood isolated from the town, but apparently it might be said of the Alexandrians that

"Exceeding peace had made them bold,"

for the approaches to the forts had gradually been built upon until at length some of the houses were even erected against the fortifications. These were the houses which were destroyed during the bombardment, and the ruin of which gave rise to the impression that the city itself had been shelled. All the forts presented the same dismal aspect of ruin. Shattered ramparts, battered casemates, huge holes in the walls of the store-houses; the heavy Armstrong guns dismantled, some with the muzzle pointed high up in the air, others lying on the ground; in all cases the gun-carriages smashed and crushed into shapelessness; burst shells, and heaps of stones and mortar lying everywhere; great deep pits in the ground, showing where an "Inflexible" shell had burst. The buildings and ramparts are of loosely-built stonework, hence wherever a shell struck, it told with full and destructive effect. Here and there one could see that a single shell had penetrated a rampart, scattered the earth, upheaved a heavy Armstrong, and enveloped a casemate in a heap of demolished masonry. In Fort Aïda an explosion, which wrecked the whole place, occurred early in the action. In the whole of the forts there were Armstrong guns of great calibre and of modern date. Their appearance after the bombardment was most extraordinary: pieces knocked out of the muzzles, huge slabs sheared out of their sides, and in many cases the coils pitted with shot marks. In most places, and at Fort Meks in particular, the muzzles were burst, but this was the work of the landing parties shortly after the action. There can be no question that the armament of these forts was of a very formidable character, and that the condition of the fleet after the encounter might have been a very serious one had the guns throughout been well handled.

After leaving the Forts we went with a friend, long resident in Alexandria, to Ramleh, the fashionable suburb of the city. The word Ramleh means "sand," and that being so it may be said that no place was ever more appropriately named. It is a mere sand waste by the shore, and its villas are separated by sand wastes. The effect is somewhat Australian, and the use of verandahs and Venetian shutters helps the suggestion. Our friend's house was close to what is known as Gun Hill, that is, where the 40-pounders were, and from his Egyptian roof he could see Arabi's advanced position and the whole of the British camp. At 4 p.m. every day it was the custom to go and see the practice from Gun Hill. Mr. A.'s house was open during the whole time, and he told us it was for the most part more like a picnic than a campaign. The officers, however, were frequently called from his billiard table by an alarm from the camp, and on such occasions Mr. A. had an understanding with them that should the English be driven in they were to warn him when retreating past his house by firing a volley through his windows! There were of course times of great anxiety notwithstanding the excitement and interest.

Mr. A. was in Alexandria during the massacre, and at the time of the bombardment he was only away two days, being the first to return to his house and live in it. While there, many of the neighbouring houses were looted. His description of the daily shooting of looters reminded one of the accounts of the latter days of the Paris Commune. Mr. A.'s garden is ornamented with heavy English shells, which, he tells his visitors, fell there—from a cart!

During the afternoon we had a stroll through the European quarter of the city, and were amazed at the destruction to be seen on every hand. The rows of fine houses, the shops, the buildings of the Grand Square, the Place Mohammed Ali, with its gardens, all a mass of unsightly ruins, from which workmen were getting out the stones and stacking them up in long rows on the footways. We had been pretty familiar with Alexandria, but in the maze of ruined stonework we were completely at a loss and could not find our way. Kalifa, however, came to our assistance, and guided by him we took a drive through the native quarter, and soon perceived that, though the destruction by incendiarism was unfortunately greatest in the European quarter, the *petroleurs* had not spared their fellows, for many native houses were burned. The extent to which property was destroyed is incredible. There must be several miles of streets in the sheerest ruin. The poor shopkeepers of the Place Mohammed Ali now occupy temporary wooden shanties, and the general aspect of this once gay and opulent quarter is wretched in the extreme.

We next day paid a visit to Fort Meks, but except that its armament was somewhat heavier than that of its fellows, there were no new features to be seen. The same desolate appearance of ruin and destruction—crippled gun-carriages, burst guns, crumbling ramparts, and shell-ploughed ground. This fort, from the accuracy of its gun practice, was the most troublesome to the fleet. The five terrible "Armstrongs," however, lay burst and useless in the sand drifts, with the rude and forgotten graves of the poor gunners round about them.

A flood of misplaced eloquence has been expended in denouncing the conduct of the British Government for having "bombarded and utterly destroyed a defenceless commercial city," and the statement has been repeated so often as to be believed by many; but I will venture to say that no one will for one moment believe it who has had the opportunity, as I have, of being conducted over the city and the fortifications by an intelligent gentleman, an old resident, who was present during the whole of the operations, and who emphatically denies that the bombardment of the forts caused any greater damage than I have described. The charge has come mainly from the advocates of peace; but it is a misfortune that such a sacred cause should be damaged by gross exaggerations, and by statements which it is impossible to sustain. The cause of peace, like the temperance cause, has suffered greatly by this habit of exaggeration.

At the *table d'hote* I sat by an English officer who had been in the thick of the fight at Kassassin, and who had escaped unhurt; he did not seem inclined to say much about his experiences on that terrible day, but he entertained a great respect for the fighting capacity of the Egyptian soldier when properly led.

During the whole of our stay in Alexandria the weather continued to be extremely boisterous and very cold, and we were glad to get on board the P. and O. steamer for Brindisi. Some Anglo-Indians joined the vessel here, and we had an opportunity of observing the way in which some of our countrymen treat native races.

A crowd of Arabs in boats were alongside, offering their wares to the passengers as they stepped up the side of the ship. Amongst the rest there was a man with his little daughter offering raw eggs, beads, shells, etc. Two of the Anglo-Indians having bought a dozen of the eggs, and having stationed themselves in a convenient position on deck, proceeded to pelt the poor trader, completely spoiling his stock, and covering him and his child with the contents of the missiles. During the voyage these fellows also behaved in a brutal manner towards the native stewards on board.

It is not to be wondered at that men like these object to judicial powers over Europeans being extended to natives, for it is probable that under the operation of the Ilbert Bill they would stand a fair chance of getting what they do not want—viz., justice. It is not difficult to imagine how such men would act towards the natives if they were a thousand miles away from a court having jurisdiction in cases of violence on the part of Europeans against natives.

Stay-at-home folks in England usually think of the Mediterranean as being calm as a lake, bathed in sunlight, and blue as the famous grotto in the Island of Capri; but such has not been my experience on the three occasions upon which I have traversed its length.

Once, however, as we were leaving Alexandria, a very beautiful phenomenon presented itself. The waters of the harbour were of a dead pale sea-green while outside the bar the Mediterranean was of an intense, opalescent, turquoise-blue, so exquisitely beautiful that the attention of the whole ship's company was directed upon it. We presently crossed the bar and dipped right into this extraordinary colour. The line of demarcation was clear and sharp, and lay just outside the harbour.

On reaching the open sea we encountered a furious gale, which continued with varying intensity until our arrival off Brindisi four days afterwards—twenty-four hours after time. The sea, which had been running high during the whole voyage, made a clean breach of the bridge on the last evening, necessitating the bringing of the vessel's head to the wind and "lying-to" for the night.

On arrival off the entrance to the harbour no pilot was forthcoming, and it began to be whispered that we should not be permitted to land without undergoing quarantine; but happily our fears proved to be groundless, and the captain having run up a signal informing the port authorities of his intention to go in without a pilot, we were soon alongside, and on European soil once again.

THE END.

INDEX.

Albatross, The	27, 115
America (*see also* United States)	135—178
America—Journey across from San Francisco	147
Albany	164
—— Schools at	165
Alkali Plains, The	155
American Language	165
André, Major	167
Appetising Mottoes and Sentiments	160
Arnold, General	167
Bill of Fare, A Curious	160
Blue Gum, The *(illus.)*	148
Brigham Young's Dominions	155
Bright, John	151
Boats	165
Bogus Ticket Sellers, Beware of	157
Buildings, Block of, Removed Bodily	161
Bull Frogs	149
Buttes, The	158
Cañons	152, 157
Cape Horn	152
Catskill Mountains	165
Chicago	160, 161
—— Fires in	161
—— Streets in, Equal to Best in London	161
—— Timber Houses still Numerous	161
—— Water Supply for	161
Churches, Opposition	167
Corinné	155
Corn over Ten Feet High	147
—— without Manure	147
Country like a Park	147
Cow-Catcher, The	154
Crash, A Tremendous	152
Descent of 8,000 feet	159
Detroit	162
Devil's Slide, The *(illus.)*	159
Dining Car, A Well-appointed	160
Dollar will Go a Long Way	168
Elevation, Greatest Attained	152
English Gold Refused	157
Eschscholtzias growing wild	147

270 INDEX.

America—Journey across from San Francisco (*continued*)
Eucalyptus, The *(illus.)* 148
Falls River 164
Fields Hundreds of Acres in extent 147
Fires in Chicago 161
Flowers, Immense patches of 147
Free Country 169
Gold-Diggings reworked by Chinese 149
—— —— Track through.. 148
Gum Tree, The *(illus.)* 148
Hotel, The Grand Pacific, Chicago 162
Hudson River 165, 167
Identification a Difficult Task 161
I guess I'll take your Gold 157
Indians, Dreadful looking 149
—— on the War-Path 152
John Scales, Justice of the Peace *(illus.)* 168
Justice, A Dealer in 168
Lake Ontario 164
Language, American 164
Life on the Road, A New Feature of 161
Lupins growing wild 147
Marigolds, Patches of 147
Military Academy, West Point 167
Mineral Wealth, Untold 148
Money-Lender complains 148
Monument Rock *(illus.)* 158
Mormon Advice 154
—— Tabernacle Visited.. 157
—— Wives lack Cordiality 156
Narrow Escape 151
Night Attack on Indians 153
Ogden 156, 157
Omaha.. 160
Pacific Railroad, A Single Track 151
Pallisades, The, Hudson River *(illus.)* 166
Passport Found Useful.. 161
Pine Forests 149
Poultry Secured by the Leg 169
Pullman Train, Life on Board 149
Railway Covered with Sheds 152
—— on Trestles 157
—— Open to Prairie 154
—— Ride, a splendid one 177
Red Sandstone Rocks 158
Ride, A Long (Omaha to Chicago) 160
Rip van Winkle.. 165
River Boats 165
—— Hudson 165, 167
Rome 164
Sacramento Valley 147

INDEX. 271

America—Journey across from San Francisco (*continued*)
Saints, Cruel Treatment by the 153
Salt Lake City Beautifully Situated 156
—— —— (*illus.*) 155
Sambo said " No Sah ! " 159
Schools, National, at Albany 165
Snow Mountains 149
—— Travelling through 157
Soil Twenty Feet Deep 147
Steamers on the Rivers 165
Streets in Chicago Equal to Best in London .. 161
Sulphur Spring.. 157
Syracuse 164
Taurus Meets the Train 154
Tennyson Claimed as an American Author .. 165
Timber Houses still Numerous in Chicago .. 161
Train, The Last Over 152
—— The, Met by Taurus 154
Trapper's Story, The 153
Turning Point between East and West 152
Utica 164
Water Supply for Chicago 161
West Point, on the Hudson 167
Witches, The 158
American Grievance 128
—— Passengers from Honolulu 127
Americans not good Sailors 127
Ascension, Island of (*illus.*) 17
Auckland 115
Avoca (*illus.*) 67
Woolgrowers 67
Australian Colonies (*see also* Melbourne, Sydney, Victoria, Tasmania, New South Wales) 101
Agricultural Labour, A Fine Field for 111
Artisans, Skilled 110
Australia, People of, Described 112
—— Young 111
Climate Exhausting 110
Ornithorhynchus paradoxus (*illus.*) 112
Drought, A Ten Months' 113
Education Amply Provided for 111
Emigrate, Who should 110
Free Trade 101
Labour Market, State of 101
—— Unskilled, A Fine Field for 111
Mining Machinery, Perfection of.. 107
Platypus, The Duck-billed (*illus.*) 112
Population 120
—— Surplus, Great Field for 110
Postal Arrangements 111
Protection 101

272 INDEX.

Australian Colonies (*continued*)
- Railways 111
- Rent of Houses Enormously Dear 110
- Schools, First-rate 111
- Telegraphs 111
- Wages Higher, but Most Things Dearer, than in England 110

Baby Hippopotamus at Play (*illus.*) 21
Ballarat 48
- Botanical Gardens 49
- Gold Mine 48
- ——— ——— (*illus.*) 49
- ——— ——— Smallness of 49
- Gold Raised 49
- Lake Wendouree 49

Bananas 127
Bay of Biscay 5
Betting on Board Ship 26
Boat in a Squall off Plymouth 2
Brandy or Whisky? 131
Brummagem Shams, where manufactured 13
Burial at Sea 131
Burying the Dead Horse (*illus.*) 21
Campbell Town 74
- Our Waiter at (*illus*) 79

Canada 162
- American Customs Officer's Equipment 164
- Clifton House, Niagara 162
- Desecration, Ruthless 163
- Green Fields like those at Home 162
- Great Western Railway 162
- London 162
- Niagara, Impressions of 164
- Paris 162
- Photographers 163
- Salary, Must Raise, I Guess 164
- Suspension Bridge at Niagara, Crossing .. 164

Centipedes, A Plague of 127
Chair, Taking the 129
Coral Reefs 116, 118
Day Dropped 119
Day Gained 119
Duel, Rumours of 121
Educated in Four Colleges 130
Egypt .. .. 181—268
- Abaid 197
- Abbaseyeh Palace 216
- Abbas Pasha 216
- Abraham or Isaac, Old Fellow like .. 191
- Aden, a Dreadful Place 239
- ——— Importance of 239

Egypt (continued)
- Adenese Women (illus.) 240
- Agricultural Operations 223
- Agriculture à la Adam 188
- Alexandria 260
- —— in Ruins 264
- —— not Bombarded 265
- —— the Forts after Bombardment 262
- Anglo-Indians 266
- Apis Mausoleum, The 203
- Arab, A Discerning 232
- —— An, Hanged 228
- —— School in Syria 211
- Arabi, Appointed Under Secretary of War .. 256
- —— at Colombo 238
- —— Bey 255
- —— Causes Numerous Arrests 257
- —— Erects New Earth-works 258
- —— How he Recruited his Army 258
- —— Made Pasha 257
- —— Military Adventurer 258
- —— Moved in a singular way 239
- —— Principal Figure in Outbreaks 256
- —— Visit to 238
- Arabi's Personal Appearance 239
- Arabs, Bedouin 183
- —— How Kept in Order 181
- —— Picturesque Party of 181
- Au Revoir (illus.) 225
- Backsheesh 185, 190, 195, 197, 198, 207, 210, 218, 224, 228, 241, [243
- —— not demanded 210
- Balah, Lake of 245, 248
- Bazaars, In the 190
- Bedrashên 201
- Beggars 195
- Bellows, not made in Birmingham 191
- Bery cheap, sah! (illus.) 191
- Bethshemish (Heliopolis) 220
- Biblical Allusions, How to Understand 185
- Biograph, A Graphic 206
- Bitter Lakes, The, Identified with Marah .. 246
- —— —— Saltness of 247
- Black Guard, A 242
- Blacking a Boy's Bare Feet 186
- Blue Jackets, Look at our de-ah 237
- Blue Ribbon Army 233
- Boat or Dahabieh 215
- Boats, How Propelled 181
- Bohemiennes 228
- Bonaparte, Attempts to Reopen Suez Canal .. 245

Egypt (*continued*)
Bond-holders, Foreign	254
Bridal Party, A	192
Brindisi	267
British Canal Shares Profitable	253
—— Mission, Schools at	211
Bûlak, A Street in (*illus.*)	219
—— Suburb of Cairo	220
Bull, The Sacred	203
Burying-ground	202
Cairo	187, 188, 242
—— Sanitary Condition of, Shocking	244
—— Trades of	188
—— Visit to, by Train	184
Camelcade, A (*illus.*)	208
Camelcades	207
Camels, Strings of	207
Carriages, Ladies'	212
Casinos	228
Cemetery, An Ancient	202
Cetewayo, *alias* The Carrib	229, 234
—— Disguised as a Gentleman (*illus.*)	235, 236
Cheops, Great Pyramid of	197
Children, Naked	208
Christian, I am a	218
Citadel, The	194
City, A great	202
Civ-il, One must be	236
Colombo	238
Colonels, The, Make further Demands	256
Concert, A Pleasant, Looked Forward to	228
Cook and Son	241
—— Name of, a Talisman	241
Coptic Guide offered a Commission	190
Coral Necklaces	227
Cotter, Lieutenant	229
Court Martial, Irregular	257
Crocodile	206
—— A dead	216
—— Lake	248
Crowd, A Motley	181
Custom-house Examination	182
—— occupied by English Artillerymen	227, 229
Dahabieh or Nile boat	215
Dancers and Howlers	210
Dervishes, The, Dancing and Howling	209
—— The, Supported by Government Endowment	210
Desert, Prayers in the (*illus.*)	209
Devils, Familiar	195
Donkey Boy, An Egyptian (*illus.*)	184
—— My Donkey, good sah	184

INDEX. 275

Egypt (*continued*)
Donkey Ride 183
—— —— across the Nile 215
Donkeys for Nine 183
—— Homeward Bound 216
—— Names of 183
—— Universal Use of 214
Dragoman (*illus.*) 182
Drive to Heliopolis .. .. ' 216
Dual Control, The 254
Dutch Hotel occupied by Royal Marines 228
Egg-hatching Establishment 194
Eggs, she only steals the Eggs now 212
Egypt, British Occupation of, how Beneficial .. 244
—— —— by whom Disliked 244
Egyptian Character, Saddest Side of 220
—— People, Requirements of 255
Electric Light, The 231
El Guisr, The Cutting of 248
Embroidery 190
End, The (*illus.*) 268
Englishman perfidious 240
English Representation on Board of Management
  of Suez Canal not large enough 252
Ethiopia shall yet Stretch Forth her Hand .. 185
European Buildings, Few 183
Exclusiveness, British 242
Excursion, A delightful 208
Ezbekîyeh Public Gardens 244
Face, A Familiar (*illus.*) 261
Fair-day, A 222
Fakir, A Holy *(illus.)* 220, 221
Fehmi Pasha 239
Fellaheen, The, ground down 259
Fort Aida 263
—— Meks 263, 265
—— Gemileh 229
French, A Nation of Retailers 252
—— Fleet, The, Withdraws 258
—— The, outwitted 240
Fresh-water Canal completed 246
Friday, the Mohammedan Sabbath 209
Gamblers on Board Ship 235
Gentlemen of the Long Robe 227
Gizeh, Pyramids of 195
—— Station 201
Goshen, Land of 244
—— Land of, preferred 244
Governor, A 'cute 239
Graphic Biograph, A 206
Graveyard at Tel-el-Kebir 243

INDEX.

Egypt (*continued*)
 Greek Money-changer 226
 Gun Hill 263
 Hassan 182, 184, 241
 —— Sultan 192
 —— —— Disguised as a Pilgrim 192
 —— —— How he Recovered his Throne 194
 Heliopolis (Bethshemish) 220
 —— Drive to 216
 Hens, Laziness of 194
 Hippopotamus 206
 Homes, Everlasting 207
 Home to Vote 225
 Hostelries 207
 Hotel Abbat 260
 Howlers and Dancers 210
 Insects something Maddening 230
 Irrigation 223
 —— Method of, Described 188
 Ismaïlia 186, 248
 Jewellers 191
 —— Weighing for 191
 Joseph and Mary's Tree 218
 Kantara 247
 Khalifs, The Tombs of the (*illus.*) 217
 Khedive's Gardens, The 215
 Khedive, The 208, 212
 —— The, Compelled to submit 255
 Koran, The, in Competition with Threepenny Pieces 189
 Labour, Forced, a Painful Sight 187
 Lady, The Last Unmarried 230
 Lake Menzaleh 230, 247
 —— Timsah 248
 Lakes, The Bitter 245, 249
 Law of Liquidation 254
 Lepère's Theory 245
 —— —— Proved Incorrect 245
 Lesseps, M., Detained at Alexandria 245
 —— Matures his Theory 246
 L'etat, c'est moi 259
 Leviathan, Job's Reference to 207
 Lucullus 259
 Lily, Painting the 186
 Luggage, A Lady's 184
 —— How Treated 181
 Mameluke Dynasty, The Last of 218
 Mamelukes, Massacre of 194
 Manufacturing Quarter 191
 Mariette exhumes the Serapeum 203
 Marines 229
 —— as Police 230

Egypt (continued)
Mausoleum, The Apis 203
Mecca Pilgrims, Rendezvous of 216
Mediterranean, The 267
—— Waters of, Flow into Bitter Lakes 246, 248
Member, Once a, always a Member 234
Memphis 202
—— Ancient, Site of .. .. , .. 201
—— Little more than a Name 202
Menzaleh, Lake of 245
Military Riot 255
Mitrahineh (site of Ancient Memphis) 201
Mohammed Ali, Mosque of 194
Money-Changers' Liberality 227
Monument, Most Ancient in the World 202
Mosque of Sultan Hassan, Visit to 194
—— The, of Sultan Hassan (illus.) 193
Mother, Son thrashes her only once a month .. 212
Mud, Great Difficulty in Making Canal 230
Museum, The National, for Egyptian Antiquities .. 222
Mutinous Conduct 256
Naval Force sent by France and England .. 257
—— —— Arrival at Alexandria 257
Nap on Deck 234
Necropolis, Ancient 202
Nile-boat, A 216
Nile, The 187
—— Valley of 188
—— View on the (illus.) 198
Nobleman, The Languishing 184
Noph (Memphis) 202
Nubians Reported to be Excellent Soldiers .. 229
Obelisk, The Oldest in Egypt 218
Octroi, or Town Tax 216
On (Heliopolis) 220
Orgies, Pious 210
Orient, The Steamship (illus.) 186
—— a Magnificent Steamship 181
Orphans, Venerable 224
Palmerston, Lord, thwarts Lessaps 246
Palms, Oranges, and Lemons 218
Patriarchal Group, A 197
Pebbles as Mementoes of Tel-el-Kebir 243
Peep, A (illus.) 190
Penny, New, Refused 185
People, Vast Numbers with Nothing to do .. 185
Perim, Island of, how acquired 239
Pious Orgies 210
Police, The, Armed with Long Spikes 216
Port Saïd 230, 247
—— a Dreadful Place to Live in 230

Egypt (*continued*)
— Harbour 231
— Lighthouse 231
— Railway wanted to 232
Power vested in Military Party 257
Prayers in the Desert (*illus.*) 209
Predictions, Ill-founded 249
President, The, of Red Ribbon Army 235
Pyramid, Ascending the Great (*illus.*) 196
— The great Step 202
— The Oldest 202
Pyramids, Road to 187
— The 216
— The, First View of 187
Quarantine 268
Ramleh 263
Ramses II., Statue of 202
Ras-el-Tin 261
Red Tape 250
— Ribbon Army 233
Rendezvous of Mecca Pilgrims 216
Revoir, Au (*illus.*) 225
Riot and Massacre of Europeans 257
Rotten Row of Cairo, The 212
Runners or Sâis, The (*illus.*) 212, 213
Sabbath, the Mohammedan 209
Safes, obviously of English Manufacture 191
Sâis, The 212
Sacred Bull, Burying-place of 203
Sakkara, To 201
Sand, A good Preservative 205
Sarcophagus, A huge 203
School, An Arab, in Syria 211
— Interrupted 189
Schoolmaster's, A, Disappointment 211
Schoolmaster, The, Abroad (*illus.*) 189
— The, asks for Backsheesh 190
Schools, Miss Whately's 211
Sculpture, Life-like 222
Selim, Sultan 218
Serapeum, The (*illus.*) 203, 204
Seymour, Admiral, Opens Fire on Forts 258
Shalouf 248
Shave, A, and a Wash (*illus.*) 199, 200
Ship of the Desert, A Wrecked 223
Shoeblacks 186
Shops Tiny 182
Shubra Avenue, In (*illus.*) 214
— — The 212
Simon Stylites 220
Soldier, British, in Egypt 242

Egypt (continued)
  Soldiers, English, quite at home 244
  —— glad to have Newspapers 230
  Sphinx, The 216
  ——, The (illus.) 199
  Spider, The 233, 234, 235
  Spider's Web, The 234
  Statue, A, Four Thousand Years old 222
  Stick, The Heaven-sent.. 198
  Story-teller, A 222
  Storytellers, Professional, at Cairo 188
  Strabo, on the Serapeum 203
  Street in Bûlak (illus.) 219
  Streets of Suez Narrow 182
  Suez 241 248
  —— Arrive off 181
  Suez Canal, A new Canal wanted 252
  —— —— British Traffic through 247
  —— —— Cost of Constructing 247
  —— —— Does not silt up 249
  —— —— Embankments of 247
  —— —— Erroneous Impressions 249
  —— —— Festivities on Opening 247
  —— —— First Undertaken by Pharaoh Necho .. 244
  —— —— French Officials inferior in capacity .. 250
  —— —— French short-sighted in Business Matters 252
  —— —— In the (illus.) 226
  —— —— Lesseps' Monopoly 252
  —— —— Lesseps, M. de 250
  —— —— Mercantile Importance of 247
  —— —— Necessity of increased accommodation .. 250
  —— —— Operations begun 246
  —— —— Palmerston, Lord, Obstinacy of .. 250
  —— —— Restrictions Absurd 251
  —— —— Ships not allowed to move after Sun-down 251
  —— —— Sinuosities of 249
  —— —— Steamers under perfect control 250
  —— —— Suggestion, A 253
  —— —— —— How to deal with Profit 253
  —— —— The 244
  Suez Hotel 182 242
  —— Streets of, Narrow 182
  Sultan, Selim 218
  Tel-el-Kebir 242, 243
  Temple, Underground 201
  Tih, The Tomb of 205
  Timsah, Lake, Lord Wolseley's base of operations.. 248
  Tomb of Tih (illus.) 205, 206
  Tombs of the Khalifs (illus.) 217
  Torture, A Novel Instrument of 220
  Town Tax, The, or the Octroi 216

Egypt (*continued*)
   Treasures, Buried 201
   Tree, The Virgin's 218
   Umbrellas, A New Use for 181
   Villages, Dreadful Mud 207
   Virgin's Tree, The 218
   Wash, A, and a Shave (*illus.*) 199, 200
   Wash Basin, An Impromptu 229
   Washing Hands, A Primitive Mode of 199
   Water-carriers (*illus.*) 215
   Weigher for the Trade 192
   Whately's, Miss, Schools 211
   What lack ye? 226
   Wild Fowl Shooting, Good 230
   Words which Broke no Bones 182
   Zagazig 187
Equator, Heat at 24
Faces too Dark to be Seen 122
Falmouth 63
   Beach and Sands 71
   Burial-place (*illus.*) 70
   Cockney Sportsman 71
   Der Dichter Spricht 65
   Epping Forest 67
   Hotel (*illus.*) 69
   Land of Snakes 64
   Magpies 63
   River Esk 64
   Stoney Creek 64
Fernshaw 53
   Hard Fare 53
   Pioneering 53
Fiji Children ask for More 117
—— Islands 116
—— Native of (*illus.*) 117
Fingal 67
Fire Brigade Practice 119
Flying Fish 27
Free Trade 99
Gambling on Board Ship 26
Golden Gate, The 131
Gum Trees, A Forest of 51
—— —— (*illus.*) 52, 53
Habits of Islanders acquired 128
Healesville 51
   A Soafler 51
   Hotel Accommodation 51, 56
   Remedy, a Sovereign 58
Hobart Town 77
   Fern Tree Valley 78
   Harvest in February 78

INDEX. 281

Hobart Town (*continued*)
  Jericho to Jerusalem, viâ Bagdad 78
  New Norfolk 78
Homeward Bound 127
Honolulu, Arrival at 122
  Baby Sold for a Dollar 126
  Breakfast ordered Overnight 122
  Brownie, Quite a 125
  Chairs or Seats usually absent 126
  Children described 124
  Country very Poor 125
  Dragon-flies, numerous 124
  Dressmaking not a difficult Art 124
  Faces too Dark to be Seen 122
  Fire-flies 122
  Flowers of the most brilliant colours 124
  Grass green and beautiful 124
  Hawaiian Islands, King of, Landlord of Hotel .. 123
  Healthiness of 127
  Heathen Chinee, his Tricks not in Vain 123
  Hotel 122
  Houses made chiefly of Rushes 126
  Islanders *en fête* 121
  Letters, Glad to be Rid of 125
  Library 125
  Museum 125
  Natives Dressed in Splendid Colours 124
  Parliament House 125
  Passenger Overboard 121
  Perfume of Tropical Flowers 122
  Pilots Decline to go out for Vessels 121
  Race fast dying out 125
  Ruth, the King's Sister (*illus.*) 126
  Servants gone Home 122
  Squatting on Ground Prevailing Custom 126
  Supper not to be had 122
  Temperature of 127
  Vegetation of 124
  Village, Native 126
  Villas Pretty and Numerous 126
  Waiters Celestial 123
  Water, Thoughts when Under 121
  Women's Clothing, Scanty 124
  Women Stately Looking 124
Honolulu, Hotel at 122
Horse, Burying the Dead (*illus.*) 21
Hotel Experiences 67
I guess the seat is dry now 129
Irish Bulls, where manufactured 13
Islanders *en fête* 121
Jefferson Brick, Junior 129

INDEX.

Jerra Jerra	96
Kandavu	115
Knife Trick, The	130
Life on Board Ship (*see* Ship—Life on Board)	3—39
Lyre Bird, The (*illus.*)	57
Launceston	61
Bees in Mourning	62
Cicadas	61
Cora Linn	63
Pomona's Temple	62
Snakes	61
Tamar River	61
Tasmanian Hospitality	62
Tonsorial Palace	62
Tree Locusts	61
Marysville	56
Stephenson Falls	56
Meal, a good square one preferred on Shore	121
Melbourne (*see also* Victoria)	39
Berry Ministry, the	43
Black Death at	40
Black Spur Mountains	50
—— —— (*illus.*)	55
Building Trade at, Depressed, Results	102
Bush, The	50
Description of	41
Education	42
Exhibition at, why decided on	102
Happy Land	46
Hobson's Bay	39, 80
Hot Winds	47
Natural History Museum	42
Old Debts, a New Way to Pay	45
Overland from Sydney	94, 100
Parliamentary Procedure	43
Parliament, Houses of	45
—— Payment of Members of	44
Protection	102
Revisited	79
Roads	50
Sanitary Arrangements, Defective	47
Stage Coaches	50
Streets wide and long	103
Tall and Fat a street sweeper	48
Tramways opposed by Cabmen	103
Vineyards	50
Yarra Yarra River	60
Mister	130
Moighty Dry	130
Native Dish called *Poi*	128

New South Wales *(see also* Sydney) ..	107
Acres Many, Men Few ..	107
Agricultural Machinery, Imported	108
Artisans Attracted from Victoria	109
Customs Revenue, Increase of	110
Employment Abundant ..	107
Exports, Increase of	110
Free Trade Colony	107
Hudson Bros., Limited ..	108
Immigration Larger than in Victoria	109
Imports, Increase of	110
Imports in 1782 and 1881	109
Industry, A Native, Created	108
Labour, Increasing Demand for ..	109
Machinery, Agricultural and Mining, Imports of ..	108
—— Mining, Demand for	107
Manufacturing Concern, Largest in Colony	108
Men Few, Acres Many ..	107
Mining Machinery, Imports of	108
—— Machinery, Perfection of	107
Policy Opposite to that of Victoria	107
Population Attracted	109
—— Constantly Increasing	107
—— Increase of, in Ten Years	110
—— Room for More	109
Prosperity, Evidences of	107
Railway System, Vast and Expanding	107
Sawmills, Steam, at Sydney	108
Shipping	107
—— Development of	109
—— During last Thirty Years	109
—— Repairing Yards Removed from Victoria	109
Timber, Native Better than Imported	108
Trade, Import and Export	107
Victoria Contrasted with	107
Oatlands	78
The Gaol	79
Pacific Ocean belies its Name	115
Parson, The, Quite at Sea ..	16
A Man of Peace now	30
Colonists' complain of	32
Congregation, Secures a ..	16
Drain Pipes, how they are made ..	30
Mixes his Degrees	31
Sermon on Geology	16
Water Pumped from a Mine Twelve Miles Deep ..	16
Passenger, Death of	130
—— falls Overboard	121
Personal Difficulties	120
—— Favour, As a ..	131
Pilots Decline to go out for Vessels ..	121

INDEX.

Protection	39, 100
Salt Water good for the " Spin-ial Orgins"	7
San Francisco	131
Baggage Master	147
Business Activity	138
—— Men, Sharp	140
Carriages, Hackney	144
Character, Bad Better than None	139
Chinaman, Am claimed as a	144
Chinese Close Shavers	141
Chinese Pigtails *(illus.)*	142
—— Joss Houses Visited	143
—— Quarter Full of Interest	141
—— Numerous	140
—— Quarter Explored at Night	143
—— Theatre Visited	143
—— Washer*men*	137
—— Wedding	143
Civilisation and Barbarism Face to Face	137
Climate Delightful	145
Correspondent, A Familiar	138
Darwin would have been Delighted	142
Dodge, A Favourite	139
Earning a Cent anyhow	132
English Fittings	137
Entrance to Harbour Sighted	131
Fire Brigades	144
Flats and Sharps	139
Golden Gate, The	131
Governor, Qualifications for a State	140
Habit, The National	138
Hackney Carriages	144
Heat and Dust Terrible	147
I Guess you are Going to England	140
Jarratt, A. J. C.	138
John Chinaman	141
Knife and Fork, only One at Meals	138
Lady Doctors Numerous	140
Luggage, Arrangements for, Excellent	147
Min-ne, Little	141
Mister, Last of *(illus.)*	146
My Wife is Dead	138
Pacific Seal	145
Palace Hotel	135—137
Police, Messenger from Chief of	139
Sea-lions	145
Seal Rocks *(illus.)*	145
Starching, a Fine Art	137
Streets, Handsome	138
Tang-y, A Chinese City	144
Tang-ye, Proof of Celestial Origin	144

INDEX.   285

San Francisco (continued)
  Temperature 145
  Tobacco Chewing and its Consequences 138
  Tramways 144
  Volunteers 144
  Yosemite Valley 146
San Francisco, Voyage to 113, 132
Sharks 18, 30
—— don't like Dark Skins 118
Ship—Life on board 3
  Albatross 27
  Bay of Biscay, Nor'-wester in 6
  Bazaar.. 34
  Betting 26, 38
  Blatant Beast, The, fires a Revolver 25
  Burying the Dead Horse 21
  Cabin'd, Cribb'd, Confin'd 3
  Cape Otway 38
  Captain not so fond of Progress as the Passengers 12
  Captains, why they are Tories 13
  Cat Chase 26
  Collisions at Sea 29
  Colonial Statesman beaten but not vanquished .. 39
  Concerts and Recitations 9
  Congregation, How to Secure a 16
  Consumptive Patients sent too late 5
  Cross-signalling.. 35
  Danite Band, The 33
  Death and Burial at Sea 15
  Dolphins 27
  Dolphin, the " Classic " (illus.) 28
  Dramatic Performance 35
  Exhibition, Fine Art 35
  Fellow-passengers 4
  First Night on Board 3
  Flying Fish 27
  Gale off Cape Leeuwin 38
  Genial Captain (illus.) advantageous 11
  German Lady, old but lively 19
  Hobson's Bay 39
  Illness of Passengers 14
  Incident in Cornwall recalled 24
  Ixion goes mad 14
  Letters Home 29
  Life Friendships formed 4
  Love your Enemies 17
  Melbourne, Arrive at 39
  Music not always harmonious 10
  Night-walkers a nuisance 9
  Nor'-wester in the Bay of Biscay 6
  Parson Mixes his Degrees 31

Ship—Life on board *(continued)*
- Pilot Fish 28
- Passengers paying their Footing 30
- —— divided into Sets 3
- Peal of Hand-bells 16
- Portuguese Man-of-War 28
- Private Convict System 4
- Quoits a selfish Game 9
- Rolling Forties 38
- Scarlet Lady 20
- Sea-sickness, Cure for 6
- Sermon on Geology 16
- Sharks 18, 30
- Ship in full Sail 29
- Short and Stout 25
- Soup too Salt 19
- Sports *(illus.)* 8
- Spurgeon's Evangelist 32
- Squall near Madeira 12
- Steward's Life a hard one 7
- Tall and Fat 25
- Tristan d'Acunha 38
- Tropical Heat 8, 24
- Tropical Phosphorescence 33
- Newspaper 10
- Water Pumped from Twelve Miles Deep 16
- Wild Spirits carry on 25
- Whale 30

Ship's Doctors 120
Snakes 61, 64, 68, 72, 73, 74, 97
Spurgeon's Evangelist 32
Steward, A Negro 115
St. Mary's *(illus.)* 68
Supper, Too late for 123
Sunday at the Fiji Islands 116
Sydney *(see also* New South Wales) 80
- Ants 90
- Bail-up 89
- Bathurst 89
- Blue Mountains 84
- Botanical Gardens 82
- Bullock Team on Blue Mountains *(illus.)* .. 94
- Bush Hut *(illus.)* 95
- Bushrangers 89
- Cottage, Mount Victoria *(illus.)* 85
- Education Act, The, Amended 92
- Excise Act 92
- Falls, The Weatherboard *(illus.)* 87
- Great Goat Sucker, The 90
- Harbour *(illus.)* 81
- Hartley Vale, Descent to *(illus.)* 88

Sydney (*continued*)
- Harvest on New Year's Day 95
- Hotels, Primitive 84
- Laughing Jackass, The *(illus.)* 90
- Lithgow 88
- Manufacturing Concern, Largest in Colony .. 107
- Oysters 83
- —— on Trees 84
- Political Situation 92
- Saw Mills, Steam 108
- Sheep Runs 95
- Southerly Buster, A 83

Sydney to Melbourne Overland 94, 100
- Albury 98
- Ants 96
- Axles, Imported 108
- Bush, The 96
- Carriage Furniture, Imported 108
- Drought of Ten Months' duration 113
- Endurance of Post-horses 98
- Euroa 100
- Free Trade at 108
- Germanton 96
- Hay, Price of 113
- Hudson Brothers (Limited) 108
- Industry, A Native, Created 108
- Jerra Jerra 96
- Kelly's Exploits at Euroa 100
- Magpies, Large 96
- Railway Rolling Stock Manufacturers 108
- Rain, Downpour of 114
- River Murray 99
- Royal Mail 96
- Sheep, Loss of 114
- Shipping during last thirty years 109
- Sighing for Old England 97
- Snakes 97
- Springs, Imported 108
- Timber, Native Better than Imported 108
- Tommy, a youthful Driver 98
- Town, An Up-country *(illus.)* 98
- Vineyards 99
- Wagga Wagga 95, 96
- Wheels, Imported 108
- Wodonga 99

Sydney to San Francisco 113, 132

Tasmania 75
- Farms large in size 75
- Good Roads 75
- Hawkers 76
- Mount Wellington *(illus.)* 76

Tasmania (continued)
   River Derwent 75
   The Rabbit and the Thistle 75
Teneriffe (illus.) 7
Travelling by Rail and Ship compared 1
Tree Ferns 52, 56
Tristan d'Acunha, Island of 36
Tropical Heat 8, 24
—— Phosphorescence 33
Tropics, In the (illus.) 40
Turtles 18
United States 169
   Americans would Become our Competitors .. 176
   Artisans (American) not Better Off than British .. 176
   —— Wages and Holidays 174
   Baggage Arrangements Convenient 171
   —— —— Described 171
   Books Dear 170
   Cabmen Disgusted 171
   Cadgers, In England such Men would be Called .. 176
   Calicoes Consigned to England 173
   Charges Simply Monstrous 170
   Children without Shoes and Stockings .. 177
   Climate more Trying than that of England .. 174
   —— of America Exhausting 176
   Competition Become Exceedingly Fierce 175
   Considerably Sold 178
   Corruption among Officials 169
   Cotton Mill Operatives from Germany, etc. .. 175
   Dear America 170
   Dinner, Charge for a Plain 170
   Engine, The Largest, in the World 172
   Exhibition, The Centennial, Philadelphia .. 169, 171
   Exports Limited by Protection 175
   Factory Operatives' Wages Lower than in Lancashire 174
   Fair Trade Agitation 174
   Fortunes, Colossal, Built up under Protection .. 176
   Freedom for Tongue and Foot 177
   Free Trade and Wages 174
   —— —— not an Unmixed Blessing 176
   —— —— under, Wider Distribution of Material Comfort 176
   Holidays Fewer than in England 174
   Hours of Labour Longer than in England .. 176
   —— —— Longer than in Lancashire .. 174
   Improvements (so-called) in Manufactures .. 172
   Labour, Honest, Avoided 176
   Liquor Traffic Presents Many Difficulties.. .. 177
   Living, Cost of, Higher than in England .. 174
   Loafers Numerous 176

INDEX. 289

United States (*continued*)
  Negro Labour does not Flood the Markets .. 177
  Newspaper Inferior and Dear 170
  New York 169
  Officials, Corruption among 169
  Over-production 173
  Philadelphia 171
  Protection, An Argument for 173
  —— and Wages 174
  —— Doomed 175
  —— Wages Steadily Declining under 176
  Railway Charges Moderate 171
  Rich, but Honest 169
  Slave Experiences 177
  Something Hot 178
  Steamboat Charges Moderate 171
  Sunday Traffic Perplexing 177
  Teetotal Lecture, A Regular 178
  Temperance Lecture, The First, they had Heard .. 178
  Tools, Inferior 172
  Wages Higher, but Balanced by Extra Cost of Living 176
  —— Higher, not a Full Equivalent 176
  —— Lower than in 1860 174
  —— Steadily Declining under Protection 176
  —— with Free Trade and Protection 174
Victoria (*see also* Melbourne) 101
  Agricultural Industries not Protected 105
  —— —— Heavily Taxed 105
  Artisans Attracted to New South Wales 109
  Books, Can Produce Her Own 104
  Cabby Overrides the Tramway 103
  Country Districts Sparsely Populated 101
  Customs Revenue Stationary 110
  Depression of Building Trade at Melbourne .. 102
  Dog Subsisting on His Own Tail 102
  Duty on Imports Demanded 103
  Exhibition at Melbourne why Decided on .. 102
  Exports, Increase of 110
  Fiscal Policy, Vicious 105
  Food, Taxation of, not Permitted 105
  Free Trade—the *Argus* 104
  —— for Raw Materials 103
  Government, Quite Right to Cheat the .. 106
  Immigration, Grants in Aid of 105
  Imported Manufactures Heavily Taxed 101
  Imports, Increase of 110
  Laws, Evasion of, by Protectionists 106
  Locomotives Costly 104
  —— Required 104
  Manufacturer's Profit not quite enough 104

Victoria *(continued)*
    Manufacturers Require Larger Field 105
    Minerals, Home Demand for, Small 105
    ——Mainly Exported 105
    Mining Industries not Protected.. 105
    —— Machinery Heavily Taxed 105
    Native Industry, In Interests of 104
    Natural Resources Neglected 102
    New South Wales, Contrasted with 107
    Population Concentrated in Large Towns .. 101
    —— Increase of, in Ten Years 110
    —— (Manufacturing) Growing Faster than its Customers 102
    —— not Retained 101
    —— Larger, a Great Want 105
    — — Room for Larger 105
    Prices sufficiently High 104
    Printed Books should be more Heavily Taxed .. 104
    Printing Materials, Suggestion to Tax 104
    Protected Industries for a Limited Time 103
    —— Manufacturers not Happy 106
    Protection Demanded by Manufacturers.. .. 102
    —— Effect on Money 106
    —— in its most Pronounced Form 101
    Protectionist Newspapers 103
    Railway Stores 105
    Shipping—Repairing Yards Removed to New South Wales 109
    Tramways Opposed by Cabmen 103
    Tariff Revision Committee 103
    Working Classes Jealous of Competition 105
    Work, Legislature Expected to Supply 102
    Workpeople very Independent 107
Voyage, Author's First, to Australia 5
Waterspout 119
Water, Thoughts when Under 121
White Squall, The 35
Yankee Journalist described 129
Yankee's Inquiry 128

REMINISCENCES OF TRAVEL

IN

Australia, America, and Egypt.

By RICHARD TANGYE.

SECOND EDITION.

Handsomely Bound in Cloth, Gilt, 8vo., 6/-
290pp. Upwards of 80 Illustrations.

Sydney Harbour.—Garden Island.

London:
SAMPSON LOW, MARSTON, SEARLE & RIVINGTON,
CROWN BUILDINGS, 188, FLEET STREET.
1884.
[All rights reserved.]

REVIEWS.

From the Rt. Hon. JOHN BRIGHT, M.P.

"I thank you much for the gift of your volume. I have read it with interest and with real pleasure. . . . It is very pleasant to see the world through your eyes and in your pages."

"Very few books of travel have appeared of late which are better compiled or in which an unobtrusive yet interesting voyage is better described than in Mr. Richard Tangye's new work, 'Reminiscences of Travel in Australia, America, and Egypt' (Sampson Low and Co.) From start to finish it is amusing, and the interest is admirably sustained; it is not only *le vraisemblable*, but also clearly *le vrai*, and we are asked to swallow no Munchausen-like tales so common in books of travel of this description. The paper, type, and sketches all combine to make the perusal of these 'Reminiscences' pleasant and entertaining." *John Bull.*

"Mr. Richard Tangye, in a well printed and well illustrated volume, writes brightly about three continents. The book is an entertaining one, full of anecdote and descriptions of places and persons. Some of Mr. Tangye's fellow travellers, if they ever recognise their personalities in his portraiture of them, will probably express themselves with warmth; but such a probability will not detract from the enjoyment of the disinterested reader in perusing this pungently-phrased synopsis of travel-experiences. The author's description of political life in Melbourne is very suggestive. Mr. Tangye's book will not disappoint those who take it up." *The Graphic.*

"An amusing little volume, full of sprightliness and good sense. . . A sheaf of adventures afloat, perfectly bewildering in their number and variety. . . . He jots down all he sees or thinks in lucid style." *Daily Telegraph.*

Readable and varied, and illustrated abundantly from clever sketches, many of them by the author himself."— *Contemporary Review.*

' These sketches are amusing. Mr. Tangye keeps his eyes open, sees what is going on, and can transfer his observations by the help of a fairly skilful pen and pencil. There is a little sketch, ' In the Suez Canal,' which, with a very few strokes, gives a capital idea of the place. Some of the figures, too, are very spirited." *The Spectator.*

"Mr. Tangye's ' Reminiscences ' have more matter in them than is usually found in a traveller's note-book. He is a keen observer and a pleasant gossip. . . . The numerous clever little sketches of scenery and incidents, by the way, greatly help out his story." *The Scotsman.*

" His book will prove a readable one to persons who may design to undertake similar voyages." *The Queen.*

" A bright and very readable narrative, by one who possesses not only business tact but who has a quick eye for the humorous and the picturesque, and who can describe very well what he sees." *Publishers' Circular.*

"Much pleasant reading will be found in this genial book of travel in well-trodden regions. Mr. Tangye heard, saw, and passed through a great deal. . . . No attempt has been made at book-making, it being simply a plain unvarnished record of personal experiences." *Daily Chronicle.*

." His pages display keen observation and kindly humour, and the interest of the reader is well maintained from end to end. . . . . The book abounds with racy narratives. It is extensively illustrated from sketches by the author and others. . . Altogether we can congratulate Mr. Tangye on a book which, written, as he reminds his readers, under many disadvantages, is thoroughly pleasant in its lighter parts, and interesting and useful where it deals with important matters."
Birmingham Daily Post.

"The author's powers of observation are ably supported by a facile pen. His description of a voyage in one of the great Australian steamers is highly interesting. His anecdotes are light, chatty, and pleasing. . . . Mr. Tangye gives an amusing anecdote regarding the political convictions of the captain. He was a Tory, as most long-voyage captains are. 'At dinner one day, happening to say I was from Birmingham, the captain said jocularly, "Oh, that's where all the shams come from!" Now the captain hails from London; but his wife is an Irish lady, so I answered, "No, captain, the things known as Birmingham shams are like the Irish bulls, and are for the most part manufactured in London." "That's so," said the captain's wife.'"
              Birmingham Daily Mail.

"The descriptions given of Victoria, Tasmania, New South Wales, and Australia generally are full of life, spirit, and interest.".
                     Midland Echo.

"Mr. Tangye has published a highly interesting account of his travels, and we have no hesitation in saying that the book will prove acceptable, not only to his legion of friends in Birmingham, but to the public generally. Mr. Tangye's diction is always smooth and graceful, his phrases are well chosen . . . an agreeable contrast to the pretentious style so much in vogue. . . . Mr. Tangye shows himself to be a keen observer of men and things, and he has a most undoubted faculty of reproducing his observations in an original, straightforward, and intelligent manner. He has also a fine appreciation of humour, many of his anecdotes being given in an exceptionally telling style. . . . . One of the most entertaining portions of the volume is that which is devoted to life on board ship. Here Mr. Tangye is seen in his happiest vein. Mr. Tangye's notes on Melbourne are exceedingly entertaining. His party left Melbourne for a few weeks' tour in Tasmania, whence they afterwards journeyed to Sydney. Mr. Tangye's reminiscences of his pleasant excursions furnish excellent and very fresh entertainment. . . . . Space will not permit of our entering into details with regard to Mr. Tangye's voyage from Sydney to San Francisco, his railway ride across the American Continent, and his tour in Egypt. We can, however, strongly commend these portions of his reminiscences as being not only very interesting, but also highly instructive. Indeed, some of his chapters on Egypt contain information that cannot fail to be useful in increasing our knowledge of the affairs of a country which at the present time is uppermost in men's thoughts." *Birmingham Daily Gazette.*

" Mr. Tangye has a happy manner of describing what he sees, and as his style is bright and terse he has produced a thoroughly interesting and readable book which will delight not only his personal friends, but also the general reader. Mr. Tangye is a good story teller, and as his sense of humour is keen he makes his narrative attractive reading. A great amount of valuable information is compressed into a small compass. . . . The incidents are picturesquely grouped. No one, we are inclined to think, could commence to peruse this book without desiring to read it through; and, judging by our own experience, a lively interest in it will be maintained from the first page to the last. The illustrations, eighty in number, by our townsman, Mr. E. C. Mountfort, add considerably to the value and attractiveness of the book. Many of the illustrations are reproductions of sketches by the author."
Midland Counties Herald.

"Bear witness to much accuracy of observation, quickness of perception, and a lively sense of humour. . . . These 'Reminiscences' are, indeed, so very agreeable, and convey in a pleasant form so much sound information, that it is not too high praise to rank them with Lady Brassey's popular ' Voyage of the Sunbeam.' They have the same merits of simplicity and straightforwardness, and the same charm of fluent, unpretending narrative." *Derby Mercury.*

" An interesting and copiously illustrated book. . . . These observations, made and recorded during a succession of foreign travel, are entitled to special attention."
Herald of Peace.

"The book contains much interesting and instructive reading, and the fact that the whole of the first edition was sold out in three weeks, and a second will be printed within a month of the first appearance of the book, shows that its popularity is likely to be very great." *The European Mail.*

"Many years ago we visited the Australian Colonies and we have never since met with so vivid and accurate a description of life on board a passenger ship and the conditions of existence in that new world across the sea as are contained in this most interesting volume. . . . Clear and incisive descriptions and racy 'bits' and anecdotes stud the pages of these 'Reminiscences.' . . . To Mr. Tangye's friends the perusal of this volume will give great pleasure; but the book has a wider purpose; its transparent truth and the solid information it contains constitute it a valuable book of reference. . . . The original sketches by which it is illustrated are clever and frequently amusing: they have been admirably reproduced by Mr. E. C. Mountfort." *The Midland Naturalist.*

"In this book we have a pleasant record of travels from the hands of an experienced traveller. . . . The simplicity of the narrative is one of its chief recommendations, and many of the opinions expressed are evidently the result of careful thought. Touches of humour abound, and here and there an apparently involuntary sarcasm makes a pleasing break in the narrative. Some of the lighter descriptions are very amusing. Thus, in the account of the company on board ship, we make the acquaintance of the clergyman who said 'he never found any difficulty in getting people to come to his church.' 'On arriving in the Colony,' says the author, 'I found our reverend friend was chaplain to a cemetery!' . . " *Nonconformist and Independent.*

"'Reminiscences of Travel in Australia, America, and Egypt' are the simple and unpretentious record of the observations made by the writer in a series of journeys made chiefly in search of health, but partly also on account of business. The record is interspersed with incidents such as befall most voyagers, and with a number of effective illustrations, which give a very pleasant life to the 'Reminiscences.' Those who take up the book will read it with real pleasure, for the observations of an intelligent man who travels with his eyes and ears open are always interesting, and Mr. Tangye shows that he can describe what he sees and hears with a ready pen."

Leeds Mercury.

"A keen observer, a lover of good stories, a clear, fluent writer, and something of an artist, he has written an exceedingly entertaining book. . . ." *The Echo.*

"The author has a keen eye, a clear perception, a ready understanding, a facile pen, and a skilful pencil. . . . He never allows our interest to flag. He takes us along with him and makes us see and hear and enjoy all the voyages and journeys for ourselves. The volume is admirably got up and ought to have a wide circulation, for it well deserves it." *Oldham Chronicle.*

"Passages of real value, because they deal with subjects on which Mr. Tangye, as a leading manufacturer and exporter, is entitled to speak with authority." *Staffordshire Advertiser.*

"A beautiful book, profusely illustrated."
Shields Daily News.

"This is no commonplace diary, but an entertaining book, containing many clearly expressed and thoughtful opinions and criticisms, much useful information, pleasing, and even touching descriptions of natural beauties, and many racy, almost rollicking, humorous stories. . . . The author is a skilful writer of clear, vigorous, undefiled English. His wide reading and his good taste have taught him what to see, and how to see it. . . . . . . Mr. Tangye tells a story from which we gather that 'Young Australia' is very similar to his cousin 'Young America.' The author says 'In one of the cities a number of young men had established a debating society, which met every

Wednesday evening in a room in a narrow street. On the other side of the street was a church where service was held at the same time. The weather becoming hot, the windows of both buildings were usually open, and the important deliberations of the young men were much interrupted by the preaching and singing in the church. With a delightful unconsciousness of what in slang phrase is called 'cheek,' they instructed their secretary to write to the minister of the church, *requesting him to hold his service upon some other evening of the week ! !* "

Walsall Free Press.

"Since the issue of Lady Brassey's 'Voyage of the Sunbeam' there has probably not been published a more enjoyable and deeply-interesting book than that of Mr. Richard Tangye's 'Reminiscences of Travel in Australia, America, and Egypt.' . . . The book is one which, once commenced, the reader is reluctant to put down until he has perused its contents to the last page, and some of the anecdotes are so exceedingly good and so aptly narrated that they will bear reading over again and again. . . . From the first page to the last the interest is fully sustained, and the book is one that we most cordially commend to the notice of our readers." *Western Daily Mercury.*

"The writer of this fascinating volume of 'Reminiscences' tells us he has made several voyages to Australia, and that he never felt the monotony so often complained of by those who make long sea voyages, 'simply because, on each occasion, he set himself something to do.' The result is a book full of entertainment and information (enhanced by well-executed illustrations), which, when once begun, the reader will not lay aside till he has reached the last page. . . . The excursions made are described in a lively manner. . . . The observations he makes upon the state of the labour market are very interesting. . . . The book is full of valuable information given in a way to awaken the reader's attention, and enlivened by anecdotes that amuse and instruct." *Glasgow Herald.*

www.ingramcontent.com/pod-product-compliance
Lightning Source LLC
Chambersburg PA
CBHW022049230426
43672CB00008B/1113